SHIPS AND SHIPBUILDERS
OF A WESTCOUNTRY SEAPORT

'Schooner *Emily Ellen* of Fowey, Peter Tadd master, off Cape
St Sabastian February 17, 1873'.

The *Emily Ellen*, Padstow-built in 1872, was registered and
owned by the Tadds, in Fowey. She was lost, with all hands, in
March 1878, while on passage for Liverpool.

SHIPS AND SHIPBUILDERS
OF A
WESTCOUNTRY SEAPORT

FOWEY 1786-1939

C. H. Ward-Jackson

With an introduction by Dr. Basil Greenhill, CB, CMG, PhD, FSA.

TWELVEHEADS PRESS

In association with the
NATIONAL MARITIME MUSEUM

1986

Cover illustration   The view from Bodinnick in 1914, looking across to Caffa Mill Pill where, on the Northern edge of Fowey town, shipbuilding had been established for many years.

The yard had been occupied by the Heller family since 1857. The last Fowey-built merchant sailing vessel, the *Rival*, had been built there by Richard Heller in 1889, and so by the time this photograph was taken the work was confined to caulking, rigging, repairs and maintenance.

Royal Institution of Cornwall.

Published by Twelveheads Press,
Chy Mengleth, Twelveheads,
Truro, Cornwall, TR4 8SN

ISBN 0906294 11 8

CONTENTS

ILLUSTRATIONS

Additional detail photographs of Fowey men on pages 2, 32, 100, 102 & 103.

2 Reuben Chappell (1870—1940) of Par who, for owners, masters and crews, painted so many of the ships that belonged to or traded into the port that he was an integral part of its life for over thirty years. Illustrations Nos. 43, 47, 60, 62, 66, 73, 74 & 85 are all of water colours or oils from his brush. Here he is seen beside the scale model he had been commissioned to make of the *Cutty Sark* in 1926, subsequently housed by the Port of London Authority and then by the Honourable Company of Master Mariners. (For his biography see *Ship Portrait Painters*, published by the National Maritime Museum).

Mr. Cecil Chappell, Par

3 About 1905, a band of Par stalwarts. From left to right: Edward Stephens (1864—1935) and Sidney Vero Morcom, both shipbrokers; Inkerman Tregaskes (born the day of the battle, 1854) who succeeded his father John as Par harbour master; — Roseveare, a boatwright at Tregaskes's yard: T.F. Pearce, bank cashier; Alfred Robins (with Service rifle) whose shire-horse hauled the clay-filled railway trucks to shipside; Richard Beckerleg Tregaskes, grocer and coal merchant; Noel Purcell, local government councillor; Captain Samuel Tregaskes, brother of Inkerman and master of the *Treffry* till he retired in 1920. Not to be left out of the picture, at far left, his little son Sidney.

FOREWORD

In the second appendix of his great book *The Rise of the English Shipping Industry* the late Professor Ralph Davis commented that — "The next advance in the history of the merchant marine may well come from the writing of substantial histories of the ports; there are none now in print". Since these words were written more than twenty years ago a number of port histories have been published, but there is still a long way to go on this particular route forward in the recording of the merchant shipping history of Britain.

C.H. Ward-Jackson's detailed history of the shipping of the Port of Fowey from the Act of General Registry of 1786 to the present day is therefore doubly welcome. It not only makes a major contribution to the maritime history of south western Britain, it is a work of outstanding quality in its field. Using the long-neglected Statutory Registration material of the port in the way pioneered in the West Country by the late Grahame Farr and by Rupert Jarvis, Ward-Jackson gives us a detailed picture of the ups and downs in the shipping history of Fowey over exactly two centuries in a way that could not be done except through a thorough understanding of the significance and potential of this very comprehensive primary source material. It is indeed appropriate that this book is being published in 1986 on the occasion of the 200th anniversary of the coming into law of the new comprehensive system of ship registry — the law which made statutory the recording of the information upon which a port history of this kind can be based.

I have had the pleasure of following the development of Ward-Jackson's work since I first asked him to undertake it, and it has been a delight to watch it mature and develop. To me it has added significance because I knew some of the men and some of the vessels about whom he writes in his last chapters. Tom Stephens, son of the great John Stephens, started the work on my book *The Merchant Schooners* by, more or less, dictating to me the first draft of the chapter in that book on the family's shipowning history. That classic vessel, the barquentine *Waterwitch*, the last British square-rigged merchant sailing ship to operate from a home port in the United Kingdom — Fowey — was a familiar of my youth, as were the *Jane Banks*, the ketch *Isabel*, the *Helena Anna* and the *Rigdin*.

Perhaps Ward-Jackson does not quite do justice to the *Rigdin*. As the Åland *Ingrid* under the pre-Revolution flag of Imperial Russia, she had sailed to the White Sea, the Gulf of St. Lawrence, the West Indies and Florida, and had been a considerable financial success. Her trouble under the Stephens ownership stemmed largely from the fact that she had been re-rigged by her first British owners (for use, very probably, as a rum runner) with the reduced sail area of a motor schooner but she had not been equipped with an efficient and sufficiently powerful engine, so, under the Stephens house flag, she made the worst of both worlds.

As for the men, perhaps the last words should be with someone who served with two of the last of them, John

1

Cockle, who was a boy seaman in *Rigdin* throughout her time under Stephens's ownership:

"Captain Beynon was like a father to me and with Jimmy Jack, the Mate, you were learning seamanship all the time. He had great patience with us two boys and would show us how to do things again and again. She was a very happy ship and a fine training ship for a youngster. They were wonderful men. Beynon's whole life was the ship and the crew. They were caring men, they looked after their crews like they looked after their ship".

What was the secret of the continued investment in vessel property in small ports like Fowey in periods when, as Ward-Jackson shows, the return on capital would seem to have been very inadequate? Part of the answer lies in the fact that the owners, or some of them, profited several times over from the vessel's operations. Shareholders who were chandlers, sailmakers, shipbuilders, provision merchants, brokers, all benefited in two or more ways from their investment and the connection with the vessel it gave them. Moreover, as C.K. Harley of the University of Western Ontario pointed out in a paper presented to the Maritime History Group of the Memorial University of Newfoundland in 1982, as long as freight rates covered the out-of-pocket expenses of operation, owners of old vessels did better by operating their vessels for what they would bring rather than by laying them up and scrapping them. Old vessels were scrapped only when the discounted present value they could reasonably be expected to earn minus their out-of-pocket costs from continued operation represented less than the anticipated earnings of the alternative investment of capital acquired by the sale of the vessel at scrap value. Old wooden sailing ships had a very low scrap value. Tom Stephens offered me the derelict *Rigdin* in 1937 for fifteen pounds — say two or three hundred at present values. This being so, why did the owning of small ships die out at Fowey a decade or more before it ceased to be a paying proposition for the people of another West Country port, Bideford? Here again John Cockle puts it very well:

"The Bar crowd (a reference to Appledore Bar which lies across the mouth of the twin Taw and Torridge rivers) were family. They were clannish, close, they worked on a different basis from the Fowey ships. They were all related, it was a tribal set up. They made money because they worked like that. The secret of success with these last sailing vessels was family operation, that and a good engine driving a screw. That's how the Bar men did it".

It is a pleasure to introduce Ward-Jackson's work. I commend it as a model for others to follow in the use of the source material so readily available for many ports in the United Kingdom.

BASIL GREENHILL
Joint Chairman,
Exeter University Maritime History Project.

PREFACE

The nineteenth century has sometimes been described as the golden age of West Country seafaring, ship-building and ship-owning and for this there is some justification as the story of each of the registry ports and sub-ports of Cornwall, Devon and Somerset will show. During the period they had much in common.

There are some fifteen or so ports of registry in the West Country, England's south-west peninsular which can reasonably be defined as the tongue of land pointing into the Atlantic from, say, a line drawn from Bridgwater on the north coast to Lyme Regis on the south. They are: Bridgwater itself, Bideford, Padstow, St. Ives, Scilly, Penzance, Falmouth, Truro, Fowey, Plymouth, Salcombe, Dartmouth, Brixham, Exeter and Lyme; each with its sub-ports that varied with the periodic alterations in the statutory port boundaries and limits.

Having the good fortune to reside in one of them — Fowey — I became interested in its history as a result of organising a modest little maritime exhibition to raise some money for a worthy village cause. Ship portraits, models and nautical relics were borrowed from old local seafaring families and, thanks to a corps of helpers, the show attracted residents and visitors alike during the holiday season of 1966.

Thus whetted, my appetite for West Country ships of the past and their builders grew to a point where in 1968 I rashly volunteered to participate in a National Maritime Museum project under which, for my part, I undertook to transcribe the Port of Fowey's Ship Registers, all extant from 1786 and, at that time, kept in the Custom House at Fowey.

At first, the task threatened to be a burden, yet gradually I became so absorbed in it that the record of almost every craft I encountered became a minor adventure. Ship registers are much more than the combined equivalent of birth, marriage and death certificates. Those unwieldly volumes, I found, are a rare repository of data regarding not ships alone but the port's people, their families, occupations, fortunes, deaths, wills, borrowings and even bankruptcies. Typed copies of my transcripts I retained for study and reference. I indexed them and, after completing the work to 1939 — it took about ten years of one-day-a-week — I abstracted, analysed, quantified and tabulated them. They provided unrivalled material for an account of the port's ships over a century-and-a-half, an account of ship-owning decline despite brave attempts to arrest it thwarted by war. Figures that clothe facts are in fashion and, though the statistician's route to the truth may be more wearisome than the poet's, there is much to be said for it. One of its faults is the impression of precision it conveys where none is possible. Figures so often depend on opinion, assumption, interpretation, attitude, method, purpose.

For example, in quantifying the rigs of vessels what was I to make of one described in 1813 as a one-masted schooner? What of another of 1806 dubbed a 'schooner brigg'? Yet another called a 'barquette' Or of numerous three-masted 'brigantines'? Were the terms over one signature really comparable with those over another? And had a ship described as 'Ripp'd up' met the same fate as one 'Broken up'? Or was it the same as 'Seized, condemned and ripped up'? Finding the answers to such questions involved opinion and assumption as well as enquiry.

In short, most of my figuring should not be read as exact but as approximation and estimate. But I do believe it makes a fair comparison possible.

It is not easy to write for the layman without offending the expert, or for the expert without boring the layman. Imprudently I have fallen into the trap of trying to address both. This has led me on one hand into more detail than might be digestible, and on the other into rounding off to the nearest ton, foot or percentage. Also I have not differentiated between those variables that, from 1836, were brought about by changed methods of measurement — notably 'old' and 'new' tons.

Unless otherwise stated, I have used gross registered tonnages to indicate the size of the vessel and, while on the subject, would risk adding that this is not a measurement of weight but of all the enclosed *space* in a ship expressed in tons of 100 cubic feet — 'ton' in this sense deriving anciently from ships measured by the number of *tuns* or casks of wine they could carry.

A further point for the uninitiated, to do with another fine, confused word: when reading and writing papers of one kind and another, even in the best regulated families error has again and again arisen from misunderstanding of the term 'port'. I have used it throughout not in its common or garden sense as a mere synonym for 'harbour' but in its statutory sense of a haven to which customs officers are accredited for the purpose of collecting or accounting for the king's customs — a port of entry, a port of registry, the bounds and limits of which are laid down by law. In this sense, of course, a port is much more widely inclusive than a harbour.

A related if rudimentary point: a port's ships are not those that trade to or from it or are even owned by inhabitants of it, but are those that are registered in it, just as a British ship, regardless of owner, is one registered in a British port and not in some other country.

To return to the thread of my narrative, it occurred to me that, by making an in-depth case study of the ships and ship-builders of Fowey I was really exemplifying what happened during the period in the West Country ports generally (with the possible exceptions of the larger ports of Falmouth and Plymouth).

In the course of supplementing my Ship Register work from other sources I came to know, almost inevitably, Dr. Basil Greenhill, author of *The Merchant Schooners* and at that time Director of the National Maritime Museum. He commissioned from me three monographs* which were published by the Museum and urged me to put into manuscript form the results of my Port of Fowey studies. Particularly for this and for his introduction to this book, the result of his encouragement, I am most grateful to him and to the *Trustees of the Caird Fund* for a generous grant which made it possible for me to complete the research work.

Acknowledgements are also due to many more people than space permits me to mention here but for his help regarding the New England schooners mentioned I must thank their leading authority, Captain W.J. Lewis Parker, U.S.C.G., (Ret'd), and for assistance regarding her grandfather, Commander the Hon. Henry N. Shore, R.N., (Baron Teignmouth), the Hon. Mrs. J. Barnwell. In making available to me the Hocken family papers Mr. John Hocken Samuel, of Restronguet Point, Truro, was of especial assistance as, indeed, were the suggestions and final typescript of my one-time secretary, Miss Anita Quick. I must, too, acknowledge the co-operation of, at Truro, the County Record Office and the Royal Institution of Cornwall; also of the Fowey Town Museum, the Mevagissey and District Museum Society, and the St. Austell China Clay Museum, as well as the patient kindness of the officers of H.M. Custom House, Fowey, during my self-imposed tour of duty there.

C.H. Ward-Jackson
Polruan,
Fowey,
Cornwall.

*The Last Log of the Schooner 'Isabella' (1976); Ship Portrait Painters (1978); and Stephens of Fowey 1867–1939 (1980).

CHAPTER ONE
SLOOPS AND CUTTERS FOR 'FREE TRADERS' 1786–1815

Fowey was the principal port of Cornwall until the 16th century. Its limits then stretched from Plymouth in the east to Falmouth in the west, its 'glorie' gained in the Middle Ages 'partely by feats of warre, partely by piracie'.

It boasted 60 tall ships in the reign of Edward III who relied on it, with Plymouth and Dartmouth, to make war for him against Brittany. It sent 47 men-of-war and transports, 770 mariners, to his aid at the siege of Calais in 1347, more than any other port. Its commanders were rewarded and commissioned as privateers and it received the same privileges as a Cinq Port. One consequence was that its people 'grew unspeakably rich and proud and mischievous'.

By the death of Henry V in 1422 it had begun to decline, and its persistent and indiscriminate plundering of ships in the English Channel put it totally out of favour by the time of Henry VIII. With the growth of Falmouth and Plymouth, in 1679 Fowey's port limits were reduced, not to be increased for another 150 years.

By 1786, when the first Ship Registration Act was put on the statute book, the condition of most of the population was, even by the standards of the time, wretched. Its ship register books are complete back to their inception on September 22 of that year, unlike many others destroyed by war or fire; and much of what appears in this monograph is derived from my transcriptions of these registers, for the National Maritime Museum, down to the outbreak of the second world war, supplemented from other sources summarised in the bibliography. The registers contain particulars of about 1,100 ships to 1939.

I have found it convenient to divide these 150 years into five periods:

1786–1815 — when most of the vessels were locally constructed, locally owned, clinker-built sloops and cutters suitable for light cargoes and much employed for smuggling.

1816–1840 — when the heavier, carvel-built topsail schooner re-opened overseas trade to the Mediterranean but adjustment to peace conditions was slow and difficult.

1841–1880 — when locally owned merchant sail (and local building) reached its peak, trading across the Western Ocean to Newfoundland, the West Indies, South America and beyond.

1881–1920 — when, increasingly restricted to coasting by competition, the port's ships were decimated by enemy action; when local ownership extended to steam but then largely died out, and the yards were confined to repairing and to building boats and yachts.

1921–1939 — when, by the outbreak of war, Fowey had only six cargo carriers and its prosperous china clay trade had come to be carried almost entirely in mechanically propelled ships, steam and motor, registered elsewhere.

THE 18TH CENTURY PORT

The coastline from the point of land called Deadman's Head or Dodman to Knaland Point, west of Looe, was long, rocky and desolate. The capital of its hinterland was St. Austell, with the big Polgooth mine close by, a growing copper and tin mining town, a smelting centre with blowing houses and new iron foundries. Its parish population in 1801 was 3,688. China clay had been discovered four miles west of it about 1750, and was being dug out of the hill farms around, air-dried and shipped to potteries in Plymouth, Worcester and Staffordshire. One early china clay freighter was the Fowey-built sloop *Hendra* of 1801, 80 tons. She was owned by Henry Lambe, a St. Austell gentleman, with Wedgwood and Bentley of Etruria, and Hollins and Warburton, Staffordshire.

Included in the port from west to east were — *Gorran*, a fishing haven with a parish population of 1,009.

Portmellon, an open cove where vessels were built ¾ mile from —

Mevagissey, then the largest coastal town in the port, its population 2,052. It had prospered especially from its pilchard fishery, so that by 1786 much of it had been rebuilt and the two arms of its new pier completed by 1780. But the American Revolutionary War hit the fishery with the first of a series of acute problems and, though pilchards were plentiful for most of the period, war from 1798 severed it from export markets, especially under Napoleon's blockade from 1802.

Pentewan nearby, where ships were beached to discharge supplies for the mines and took away ore and the locally quarried stone.

West Polmear, another beach where supplies were landed for St. Austell. Here Charles Rashleigh, a St. Austell attorney-at-law, started building a harbour in 1791 to serve St. Austell, completing it ten years later, during which the population grew from nine to 300. He re-named it Charlestown.

East Polmear, on the east shore of the Par River estuary, another place where ships were beached for loading and discharging. At low tide the whole estuary was a bank of sand and silt, created by inland refuse washing down and pushing the coast into the sea. Par as a harbour had not yet been built.

Polkerris, another fishing hamlet near Menabilly where the Rashleighs lived.

Fowey, around the Gribben headland from the bays of Mevagissey and Par, on the estuary of the River Fowey. It had the only other deep water harbour than Falmouth in Cornwall, landlocked and taking vessels of up to 1,000 tons at all times of the tide, busy with merchantmen, watermen, occasional ships of war, and salmon seines. It was the port's most distant harbour from St. Austell, a disadvantage that restricted it till the coming of the railways. Fowey Town was the port's administrative centre where the Custom House was, and the pocket borough of the Whiggish Rashleigh family. The population at 1,155 was a great deal less than that of Mevagissey.

Polruan, another fishing village, on the east bank of the harbour and its maid-of-all-work as it is today. Its population was then 678.

Lostwithiel, six miles up river, taking timber, salt, limestone, sand and coal for the farms and mines inland, its population 743.

The main outward traffic of the port included mineral ores, building stone, salted fish, grain, china clay; the inward traffic the necessities of mining, fishing and farming. Its people were predominantly fishermen, mine workers, seamen and farm labourers, plus the ancillary tradesmen and craftsmen. Transients were numerous — Welsh, Irish, Channel Islanders, Bretons. For most people in the area the years we are dealing with were 'starving times' when the poor were often reduced to living off limpets. With minority exceptions, the State and its church were hated.

The State was hated especially for its duty on salt which the Cornishman used to cure the pilchards for his family. One bushel of salt was needed to cure a thousand pilchards, which was a good deal less than most families needed for the winter. And the duty on it often represented half a fisherman's income in a poor season. So the only way he could get cheap salt was by smuggling it. Also he was under permanent threat of impressment into the Navy, resulting in his boat and nets being idle and going to rot. The Church of England he hated because it was part and parcel of the State and levied fish tithes on him. Most Cornishmen were dissenters, usually followers of John Wesley, who was in St Austell in 1785. It is hardly surprising that many supplemented such little lawful income as they had by recourse to unlawful means, undeterred by Wesley and the religious revival in progress at the time.

A high proportion of the vessels registered at Fowey were engaged in smuggling. Many were built for this purpose, notably at Mevagissey where the vagaries of the pilchard fishery particularly encouraged illegal trading. The high import tariffs, raised again and again to pay for war, made the profit potential for smuggling very tempting indeed, although it was always the master smuggler — the organiser and financier — who took the lion's share. English gold guineas commanded a high premium on the Continent, and a profit was forthcoming even when two out of three ships were lost. The port, too, was only a hundred miles from Guernsey whose merchants specialised in supplying suitable goods, selected, stored and packed for the purpose.

Until 1802 the registers usually state the place where each ship was built but thereafter they begin to say 'Within the Port of Fowey', so that when 'Fowey' is specified it is not clear whether the town or port is meant and, indeed, from other indications one may be sure that the town is only sometimes meant. Nevertheless, it is not difficult to tell from the registers that the smuggling fraternity concentrated mainly on Mevagissey. In those days Mevagissey and St. Austell bays, obscured beyond the Gribben headland, were poorly guarded and a favourite place for landing goods.

In Fowey Town there lived a dozen or so naval officers and a substantial Custom House staff. In 1791 the Surveyor was Alderman William Cotton, succeeded in 1795 by Robert Flamank. The Controller was H. Couche. John Kimber took over as Collector from John Courts in 1799. In addition, there were 3 Custom House

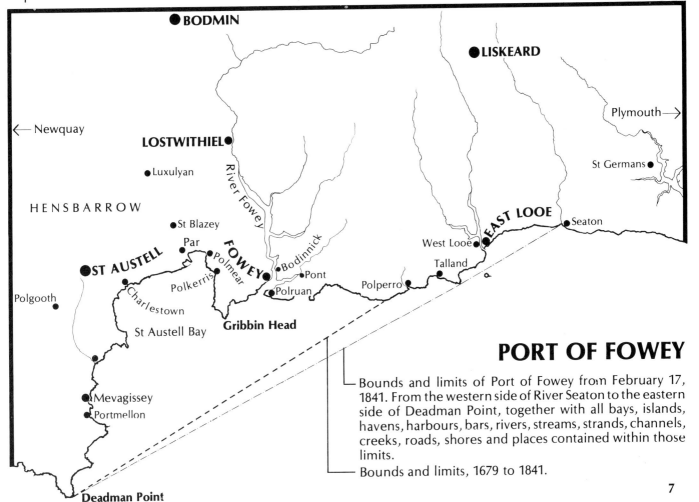

PORT OF FOWEY

Bounds and limits of Port of Fowey from February 17, 1841. From the western side of River Seaton to the eastern side of Deadman Point, together with all bays, islands, havens, harbours, bars, rivers, streams, strands, channels, creeks, roads, shores and places contained within those limits.

Bounds and limits, 1679 to 1841.

7

officers, 1 land waiter, 3 salt officers, 1 searcher of salt, and 1 Excise officer. Riding officers called at frequent intervals; they, with the Customs & Excise, patrolled ashore, and the Revenue Cruisers afloat. The premises on Custom House Quay were not then used for the purpose; they were occupied later in the 19th century. The stable is still there in which the dragoons sheltered their mounts.

A watch-house on what has since been called Point Neptune scanned the harbour entrance, the approaches to which were defended by batteries totalling 21 guns, shown on the chart first published in 1786 from a survey made by Lieutenant James Cook, R.N., oldest of the great explorer's three sons. St. Catherine's Castle, overlooking the harbour entrance, built by Thomas Treffry in Henry VIII's time, was armed but the two blockhouses on either bank dating from the 14th century were long since in ruin.

Fowey had long been a notorious smuggler's resort, one of the fourteen places around the coasts where Customs sloops had been established in 1698; but as well as reducing the number of riding officers, war necessitated the detachment of Revenue Cruisers as naval auxiliaries. Meanwhile, higher duties brought the greater temptation of yet higher profits. By about 1800 it was conservatively estimated that in the country generally, over 300 vessels were permanently engaged in smuggling and that over 20,000 people gained their livelihood fulltime from what they simply called 'The Trade'.

KIND AND SIZE OF SHIPS

On the Fowey register as at December 31 1792 there were 52 vessels (plus 4 others entered in the last twelve weeks of that year not included for some reason in the non-statutory annual lists of the Registrar General of Shipping and Seamen). Their tonnage totalled 2,374, averaging 46 tons; and their employees were 214 men and boys, an average crew of 4 per vessel. During the previous seven years some 60 vessels had ceased to be registered at the port, 23 having been transferred (especially to Guernsey), 14 lost, 10 seized and condemned for smuggling, *etc*. The relative importance of Fowey shipping at this time may be seen from the equivalent figures for other West Country ports: Bristol had 307 vessels averaging 124 tons, Dartmouth 284 (46 tons), Plymouth 114 (55 tons) and Falmouth 48 (86 tons).

What kind of vessels were Fowey's? In considering this we are up against non-use at the time of strictly standard terms — practice varied as between merchant marine and Navy, from one port to another, one time to another, from one Surveyor to another, an obstacle to analysis that is lessened but not eliminated by the care with which the Fowey ships were described in the registers. Also rigs were altered from time to time (calling for *de novo* registration), so that for my analysis

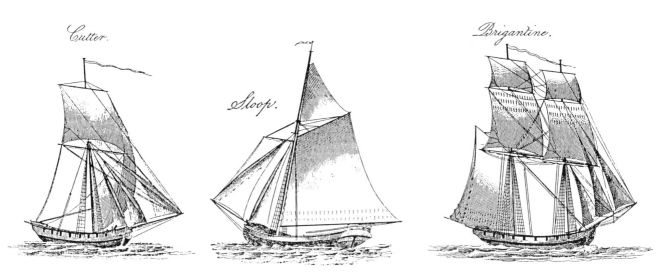

Cutter. *Sloop.* *Brigantine.*

at Appendix 'B' I have used only the initial description of ships so altered.

Sloops were the largest class, and the next most common were cutters. The first cutter does not appear until 1798. By later standards there is not a great difference between a cutter and a sloop; and the description 'Cutter fitted as sloop with standing bowsprit' is frequent. What is certain is that over 60% of ships registered were called sloops or cutters and mostly they were of clinker construction.

These vessels could be conveniently beached to load and unload cargoes and were the principal craft used for smuggling — fast, handy, manoeuvrable, economic. They were defined as furnished with one mast, the main-sail of which was attached to a gaff above, to the mast on its foremost edge, and to a boom below, by which it was shifted to either quarter. The sloops differed from the cutters by having a fixed steeving bowsprit and a jib-stay; nor were the sails generally so large in proportion to the size of the vessel. The cutters had a bowsprit that could be run in on deck.

However, the registers from 1798 refer to these vessels as having 'a legal stay', being 'legally equipped', or 'cutter fitted legally as a sloop'. These descriptions reflect the complex regulations that were imposed upon designs and rigs that could give smuggling vessels speed and resistance advantages.

Early legislation had been strengthened by an anti-smuggling Act in 1779 when ships of under 200 tons carrying goods in illegal packages became forfeit, and when boats with more than four oars were forbidden. After an Act of 1784 'all vessels belonging...to any of His Majesty's subjects, called cutters, luggers, shallops or wherries' were forfeit as smugglers unless they were square-rigged or fitted with a standing bowsprit or a standing jib-stay of reasonable size. They were forfeit if their bowsprit was longer than two-thirds of the distance, measured along the deck, from the foreside of the stem to the after side of the stern-post. Unless square-rigged or a sloop with standing bowsprit no vessel of any kind was allowed to be clinker built. To what extent Fowey's ship-builders and their clients avoided or evaded the consequences of such restrictions is a matter for speculation.

The sloops and cutters averaged about 58 tons. From 1794 the size tended to increase, with the addition of various cutters of 100 tons or more. The largest was the 167-ton *Mars* (1798), clinker built at Mevagissey, altered to a brigantine four years later and sold to Liverpool. Others were almost as large — the *Swift* (1799) of 164 tons, also altered to a brigantine, and the ironically named *British Constitution* (1800), 156 tons, 'seized, condemned and publicly sold at Fowey, October 23 1800'.

A smuggling craft more typical of the place and time

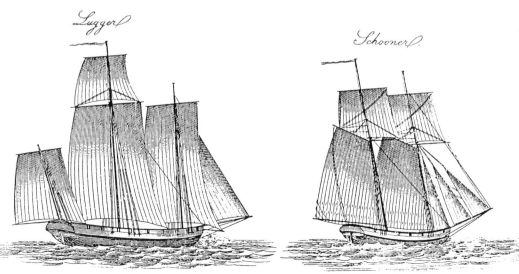

5 Rigs of the period c. 1800.
Falconer's 1815 Marine Dictionary

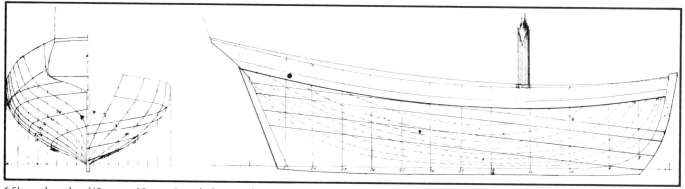

6 Sheer draught of '*Ferrett* of Fowey Smugler'; built at Plymouth, seized for smuggling, condemned and sold 1805 at Bristol where her lines were taken off by R. Hilhouse, shipbuilders.

was the *Jane* (1796), built at Mevagissey and owned by Thomas Shepheard, a shipwright of that town, her master John Farran. She measured 48'8" × 17'10" × 8'5". Her tonnage was 56, and she was described as clinker built, a square stern sloop with ten port-holes. She too was seized.

As far as I know, no draught exists of a Fowey-built cutter or sloop of the period, but the Science Museum does have a photograph of a draught of 'The Fowey Smuggler *Ferret*' (illustrated). She was registered on October 12 1803 as built in Plymouth in that year, square sterned and 'fitted as a sloop with a standing bowsprit', legal stay and 10 ports. She was seized and condemned, carried into Bristol and sold there in 1805. Her owner was John Drew, a Mevagissey mariner, her master William Harris. Her tonnage was given as 44 $^{59}/_{94}$ths, measurements 44'11" × 16'4½" × 7'2½".

This draught of the *Ferret* was included in a collection of plans from Hilhouse's yard at Bristol lent to the Science Museum in the 1930s. From the same collection we do have a draught of a Fowey-built lugger, the *Lottery* of 1805 to which I will refer later. There were 26 other luggers registered during the period, all three-masters like the *Lottery*. They averaged 77 tons. Few were undecked, several were over 100 tons. They were nearly all built locally and included two that were probably for privateering, quickly transferred to Guernsey by their owners. They were the *Speedwell* (1794) of 266 tons, built at Polmear with stanchions for four guns on the fo'castle and for twelve swivel guns; and the *Zephyr* (1794) of 56 tons,

with stanchions for four fo'castle guns and for eight swivels.

Brigantines were as many as 47; the first craft described as a brig did not go on the register till 1802. The largest brigantines were the Fowey-built *Speedwell* of 1802, 151 tons, and the 135-ton *Prosperous Mary* (1793) built at Kingsand, Dublin. Otherwise the brigs and brigantines were locally built or were small prizes, usually sold elsewhere; several were taken by the French, and only two were seized for smuggling.

Of the 32 schooners in Appendix 'B' 26 post-dated 1802 prior to which this rig was hardly in use and only on small fry about 40 feet in length, say 35 tons. Only in the last ten years of the Napoleonic wars did schooners even begin to grow in number and size. Also where there was only one full-rigged ship (of 157 tons) prior to 1803, by 1815 there were four averaging 258 tons, as well as a barque of 239 tons. These changes may reflect greater confidence in the safety of our merchantmen after Trafalgar although vessels of upwards of 200 tons rarely stayed long with Fowey.

The 37 barges and lighters may have included some that were sloop-rigged but not so described. Also a number were Plymouth built but the biggest was 'Built within the Port', and a note of pride may be detected in the record. She was the 70-ton *Charlestown* 'Of Charlestown in the Port of Fowey', registered 1795 when Charles Rashleigh was constructing the harbour at West Polmear. She was almost certainly from the yard of Thomas Shepheard, her initial owner, who sold shares in her to Joseph Dingle, merchant, and to

7 Model of a Fowey revenue cutter, bought in
Fowey in 1935. Its somewhat rounded stem,
rockered keel and raking sternpost are typical
of the period c. 1800.

Richard Williams and John Nancollas, mariners of St. Austell.

The *Charlestown* was in service out of the port longer than any other vessel I could find in the period — fifty-five years. From 1824 she was described as a sloop and in 1850 'went absent'.

These barges and lighters were often engaged in the conveyance of limestone from Plymouth to the kilns of the south Cornish creeks, the closest they could get to the sour farmlands, as well as in construction work in progress on the coast — at Charlestown and on the great breakwater at Plymouth Sound, commenced in 1812, finished 1848.

One oddity of the period was the galliasse *Thomas*, 153 tons, formerly the *Anna Maria*, a prize taken from the Danes. She was bought by a Fowey merchant, William Norway, who quickly sold her to Plymouth.

The average size of all 441 vessels that went on the register between 1786 and 1815 was about 68 tons, not very much larger than the sloops and cutters. And of course many ceased to belong to Fowey from being lost, seized, transferred, *etc.* Most of them are recorded as being built in the port.

THE BUILDERS

I have summarised the places of build at Appendix 'D' from which it will be seen that 68% came from the port's own yards. Together Cornish and Devon yards provided as many as 82%. Plymouth, the nearest port of large size to Fowey, provided more than all the others from Devon together. The next largest source was Enemies of the Crown: 47 prizes of war taken from the French, Danes, Spaniards or Prussians were bought by local people, most of them having been brought into Fowey and put up for auction.

Unfortunately the name of each ship's builder is only occasionally registered; but where the name of a ship-builder or shipwright occurs among the initial owners it is reasonable to assume that the vessel concerned was built by him where his address and the place of build coincide as they usually do. From the registers it is thus possible to arrive at some idea of who built over half the vessels known to have come from local yards.

At the same time the outputs given below and at Appendices 'C' and 'D' should be treated as estimates rather than of certain record, but I believe them to be a reasonably reliable indication of the builders' *relative* outputs.

In this 1786—1815 period, when the port met most of its needs from its own yards at Mevagissey and on Fowey harbour, the builders were:

Place	Builder	No. of vessels	Average size to nearest ton
Mevagissey	Thomas Shepheard	60	74
	James Melhuish	20	76
	James Dunn	17	90
	Peter Smith	5	113
	James Furse	1	25
	John Allen	4	75
	William Forsyth	3	62
Fowey	Thomas Nickels	30	77
	John Wilcock	10	59
	Richard Poulgrain	2	99
	William Brokenshaw	1	101
Polruan	William Geach	6	40
		159	75

In this 30-year period of wars with France and America it appears that more shipping, in both numbers of vessels and aggregate tonnage, was built in the port that at any subsequent time, and probably the main causes were the demands of the smuggling trade and of privateering, both of which declined sharply after reaching a peak in the late 18th century. Concurrently the port's builders probably supplied more vessels direct to other ports than they did subsequently — output that does not show up in any of these figures. The Mevagissey-built cutters and sloops were much sought after by the Trade elsewhere.

Indeed the Mevagissey output is shown by the above figures to have been considerably greater than that on Fowey harbour, with Thomas Shepheard by far the most productive. He was already at work by 1786 and turned out about three vessels a year from 16 to 266 tons, a wide range. Wherever it was exactly, his yard was less than he needed as, in 1794, he built the big *Speedwell* lugger on the beach at Polmear, and then four much smaller craft in the same place, ceasing work there in 1798 when Charles Rashleigh was completing the construction there of Charlestown harbour.

Shepheard seems to have been the principal builder, especially for the smugglers: 9 of 60 of his vessels were seized, 19 were transferred to Guernsey and 4 went to

Rye, another port notorious for its involvement in the Trade. He died about 1812, his output ceasing two years previously. Peter Smith then appears as a builder, and it is not unlikely that he was Shepheard's successor.

When John Allen stopped building in 1800 James Dunn, related to him, started up (at Portmellon) and he and his family continued into the 1840s. James Melhuish was launching about one sloop or cutter a year between 1787 and 1804, but his name then ceases to occur.

At Fowey, Thomas Nickels was also already working by 1786, and his successor George Nickels continued the business from 1821 until 1865, the port's longest ship-building tradition. By the end of the Napoleonic Wars Thomas had been responsible for an output at a rate of about one-and-a-half vessels a year of sizes as varied as those of Shepheard at Mevagissey. These included ten of over 100 tons apiece and, for some London merchants, a 308-ton full-rigged ship, *Twins* of 1803.

Nickels also built for the Navy Board, the 50-ton sloop *Fowey* (1795) and the brig *Primrose* (1806) 18 guns, stationed on the coast of Spain 1807 and wrecked on the Manacles 1809 going to or coming from the Peninsular with troops.

John Wilcock's clientele appears to have been much the same as Shepheard's and Nickels'. Four of the ten he built between 1793 and 1805, mainly sloops and cutters, were seized. On the east bank of Fowey harbour, at Polruan, William Geach turned out a few small vessels and continued to do so through the first forty years of the 19th century.

THE OWNERS

Like most merchant craft of the time, the majority of these vessels were owned by assorted traders, craftsmen and mariners, from one or two to half-a-dozen or so people, often closely related, the number usually rising with the size of vessel — people whom the builder or other original owner interested in taking shares to spread the risk. Vessels with one owner for any but a short period were usually below average tonnage.

The registers state the name, occupation and address (town, village, parish or port) of each 'subscriber' (i.e. owner who affixes his signature) and 'non-subscriber', and only exceptionally is there any indication at this period of the extent of each person's interest — e.g.

'half-share'. It was not until 1824, when the division of each ship into 64ths became statutory, that the number of shares held is always specified.

A random sample suggested the following rough order of ownership by occupation:

Mariners	33%
Shipwrights & ship-builders	12%
Tradesmen catering to ships — victuallers, ropers, sailmakers, blacksmiths, *etc*	12%
Fishermen	2%
Coopers	4%
Innkeepers, brewers, maltsters	4%
Miscellaneous tradesmen — tailors, grocers, mercers, *etc*	6%
Merchants	6%
Yeomen and farmers	4%
Professional men — surgeons, doctors, attorneys, *etc*	3%
Gentlemen	9%
Miscellaneous	5%

One may say, then, that the owners were about one-third mariners, one-third others whose income was derived from the sea, and one-third a general assortment. Of all owners about 90% lived in Cornwall, overwhelmingly in the St. Austell/Fowey area and another 7% lived elsewhere in the West Country, particularly the Plymouth district. Very few were in London or Bristol.

The tradesmen concerned in the building or fitting-out were no doubt often part-owners, probably taking part of their due in shares. A typical example is John Hugo, who lived at the Sign of the Ship, Mevagissey, variously described as following three occupations closely connected in a seaport: inn-keeper, blacksmith and anchor-smith. He had shares in upwards of 15 vessels between 1786 and 1802, most of which were built by Thomas Shepheard. From 1785 for many years the Mevagissey Harbour Trustees met at Hugo's house to transact their business.

Ownership by Quakers seems normally to have been recorded, the only religious persuasion noted, perhaps because of their conscientious objection to bearing arms. There was a community at St. Austell but only two ships had owners 'Being of the People Commonly Called Quakers', as it was put.

8 Captain James Dunn of Mevagissey, master mariner, shipbuilder, shipowner and smuggler.   *Mevagissey & District Museum Society*

THE MASTERS

At this period the names of masters are usually given in the registers, sometimes only one or two per ship over a number of years. Sometimes there is a string of names, usually with the date on which command was taken and where it was taken. The record of where a new master took over is a handy indication of where the ship traded.

A noticeable number of names among the shipmasters are Welsh: Evans, Williams, Thomas; some are French — Fleur, Colinette, le Cronier, Lelean, Lukey (anglicised Lukis). Many indeed are local names still well-known in the St. Austell/Fowey area: Allen, Banks, Barrett, Climo, Cock, Court, Dunn, Dyer, Farran, Furse, Geach, Hicks, Hunkin, Jago, Johns, Jolly, Langmaid, Libby, Ley, Nancollas, Pearn, Quiller, Rowse, Rowett, Salt, Slade, Stephens, Tadd, Tippett, Wilcock.

Ball was the name of one typical family of masters at this period. Ambrose Edward Ball, Mevagissey gentleman, had shares in the *Favourite* (1787), the *Brothers* (1792) and the *Brittania* (1801). James Ball is given as master of four ships, William Ball of three, Thomas Ball (of Cawsand) of four. Luke Ball was a Gerrans fisherman, Philip the Younger a Mevagissey merchant. It was probably not inconvenient for the family that Philip Ball in 1785 was appointed at twelve guineas a year to the combined offices at Mevagissey of Quaymaster and Collector of Duties.

While the stated occupations are no doubt the correctly described colours, so to speak, flown by each individual, it would be wrong to assume that they were the only income source. Grist for the mill came from wherever it could be garnered. A mariner would till the soil; an inn-keeper would farm; a fisherman might work as a shipwright. This is truest of the least skilled, lower paid occupations, and of those that were seasonal or affected by weather (that is, of most of them). The chief 'black economy' occupation was, of course, smuggling, the Trade, or connected with it — 'moonlighting' literally.

THE SHIPS' FATE

So far we have considered the port itself, its trades, the number and kind of its ships, its builders, owners and masters. What happened to its ships? At Appendix 'C' is an analysis of the fate of the 441 vessels registered in the thirty years ended 1815, from which it will be seen that as many as 47% of them were transferred to other ports, a high figure that reflects the large sale elsewhere by the port's builders of a substantial number of their sloops and cutters.

Of the 59 that were transferred to Guernsey a number, unknown but probably more than a few, were used in privateering, in which the island was heavily engaged: many of their privateers were quite small. Also a relatively limited number of Fowey vessels — only 15 — were taken by Enemies of the Crown. They were: *Prince of Wales* (of 1791); *Diligence, Sophia*, and *Five Brothers* (1793), *Charlotte* and *Vertumnus* (1797); *Happy Society* (1800); *Seven Brothers* (1801); *Mary Ann* (1803); *Virtuous Grace* (1804); *Four Sisters* (1805); *Rebecca* (1807); *Johanna* (1810); *Phebe* and *Mars* (1813).

The register of the 65-ton sloop *Johanna* notes that Thomas Kitto, master, on February 3 1815, six weeks after peace had been signed ending the War of 1812, reported that she had been taken by 'the American schooner *Macedonia*' — probably the *Macedonian*, sharp, narrow, fast sailing frigate built in 1812 for the King's Navy but captured that year by the *United States*, 38 guns. The biggest loss was of the full-rigged ship *Virtuous Grace*, 235 tons, owned by a Fowey merchant, John Kelly Graham, to the French in 1806.

Anti-smuggling legislation in the 18th and early 19th centuries failed to achieve its purpose largely because it coincided with other legislation that raised duties and therefore the possible profits to be made from smuggling. Also the Authorities were so deprived by war of resources for combatting the Trade that it was carried on with minimal interruption.

Scouting by the Revenue Cruisers was not very thorough in the seas through which the Cornishmen carried their contraband, mainly from Guernsey — through the western English Channel, to both south and north coasts of Cornwall and Devon, to Wales and Ireland. On paper there were 37 Customs and 7 Excise vessels patrolling the coasts of England and Wales, but west of Poole they were infrequent, while Cornwall had only one 'seizing' port that mattered, St. Ives.

SEIZED FOR SMUGGLING

It is remarkable then, that over the period 1786—1815 as many as 81 Fowey vessels are recorded as having been seized for smuggling, and destroyed or sold as a consequence — that is, 18% of all those registered. And that is not counting others baldly described as 'Ripped up'. Indeed, up until 1802 the seizure percentage ran to nearly 23%.

These rates relative to those of other ports must have been unusually high, despite the smugglers' advantages. After all, they had fast vessels that were locally built especially for their needs, and masters and crews with an intimate knowledge of the western seas and coastlines. Also they and their backers appear to have used the most ingenious tricks to achieve their ends. It is, for instance, hard not to suspect that confusion of the Revenue was one motive in the naming of some vessels in those days before nomenclature regulations were introduced. In the period under consideration there were at Fowey no less than 16 vessels called *Betsey*, 13 called *Mary*, 8 *Fowey*, 7 each of *Endeavour*, *Fortune*, *Hope* and so on.

The West Country maritime historian, Grahame Farr, pointed out that the registered descriptions of the Fowey vessels were unusually detailed and that they must have been very helpful in the war against the smugglers. Directly any vessel was reported loading spirits or other suspect goods at a port across the Channel her description was sent to all Collectors of Customs so that the Revenue cutters could be warned to look out for them. Thus, the *Happy Return* of 1800: 'Square stern cutter, clinker built, fitted as a sloop with steeved bowsprit and legal stay, a knee at the stem, not deep waisted but with stanchions and rails'.

Such careful descriptions coincide especially with the handwriting on the registers of Robert Parker Flamank who signed as the officer responsible from January 1795 to June 1822. He was confirmed in the rank of Surveyor in 1805 prior to which he had served for thirty-two years as Deputy Searcher and Land Waiter. He was of an old Bodmin family but was not the Robert (1768—1847) who became mayor of that town in 1826.

All told Flamank was a Customs Officer for almost fifty years, all at Fowey. Superannuated on £150 a year in 1822 — a good pension in those days — he was a Justice of the Peace, and *Pigot's Directory* for 1823 and 1824 described him as Stamp Officer at Fowey, another position of trust, responsible for the issue of Government stamps and the receipt of stamp duties, Excise and other taxes, then separate from the Customs. Thus, Flamank was a conscientious servant of the Crown, and it is likely that he had much to do with the high seizure rate.

With seven times more vessels seized for smuggling than were taken by the King's enemies, the number of others so engaged could hardly have been few. Their owners, crews and shore helpers must have involved a large part of the population, if not the greater part. And Guernsey, as well as being the smugglers' principal source of contraband, was also by far Fowey's best customer for ships. As many as 59 of the 209 Fowey vessels transferred to other ports went to Guernsey.

The registers show, in short, that some 32% of all Fowey ships between 1786 and 1815 were either seized for smuggling or were sold to the home of the smugglers' suppliers and backers.

9 The sinking stones were always bent on, and kept on deck till just before slipping.

This was a reciprocal trade that did not extend to the Channel Islands as a whole. So far as Fowey is concerned, it was the preserve of Guernsey. Jersey neither appears in the registers as a place at which new masters were appointed to Fowey vessels nor as the address of any owner or master. Also over the whole thirty-year period while some three score vessels were sold to Guernsey only three went to Jersey.

The most powerful supplier and employer of the smugglers was Carteret Priaulx and Company, whose papers (1740—1840) are preserved in the Priaulx Library at St. Peter Port. The largest commercial house in Guernsey at the time, the firm was built up by Thomas Priaulx the Elder, and directed from the 1780s by his three sons, Carteret, Thomas and Anthony, heavily engaged in privateering and in supplying goods to the mainland.

THE GUERNSEY CONNECTION

The influence of the Guernsey connection on the ships at this period calls for an extended attention to it, especially as it was largely illicit and thinly documented. What follows regarding it is largely from a paper I read in 1969 at an Exeter University economic history seminar.

Smuggling into Britain was facilitated by the development of the fore-and-aft rig, permitting ships to go in and out on the same wind, an advantage denied to the square riggers. It expanded in proportion to the increase in import and Excise duties, raised to an unprecedented extent in the 18th century. Heavily

11 (a) Method of slinging tubs, and (b) mode of carrying tubs.

taxed commodities of small weight and bulk relative to value lent themselves to smuggling — notably wines and spirits, tea and tobacco. The greater the duty the greater the temptation to try to evade it.

The West Country smugglers came to obtain their main supplies from Guernsey from various causes. When in 1689 Guernsey's ancient privilege of neutrality was withdrawn, the islanders fitted out privateers against the common enemy, France. The captured cargoes were Guernsey's first high value exports, and the resultant capital enabled the islanders to push trade with England, sixty miles away. They imported wines and spirits and stored them in their vaults and caves, ideal for maturing purposes and developed by the Bordeaux merchants whose own storages were poor. A system grew up whereby the Guernseymen bought in bulk and shipped out in smaller casks for all comers who could pay. The establishment and extension of the bonding system on the mainland, which undermined their 'legal' trade, caused them to turn more and more to smugglers for custom.

So the island became the principal depository of spirits purchased by the West Country smugglers, and the business so flourished that its numerous vaults became inadequate and fortunes were made even by the coopers. St. Peter Port, like Mevagissey, was largely rebuilt at this time from the proceeds.

The English Government sought to impose Customs officers on the island, notably in 1736 when the Smugglers' Act was passed, and in 1767. This encouraged the French to make Roscoff, a village on

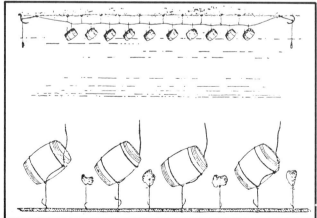

10 (a) Method of securing tubs and stones for sinking, and (b) a crop sunk.

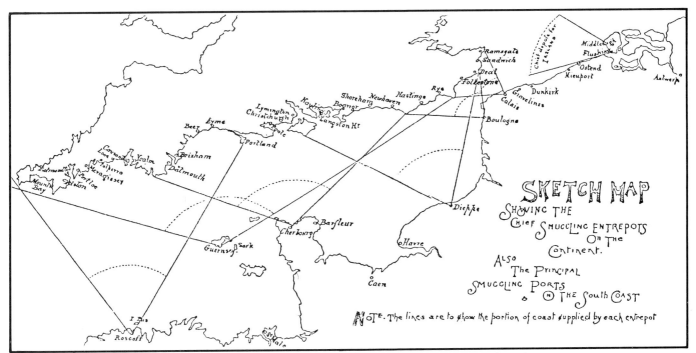

12 Map from *Smuggling Days & Smuggling Ways* (1892) by Commander the Hon. Henry N. Shore RN (1847—1926), afterwards 5th Baron Teignmouth. Illustrations 9, 10, 11, 14 and 16 are from the same source.

the Finisterre peninsular, a free port in anticipation of Guernsey becoming unable to continue its trade, which provided them with gold that commanded a premium on the Continent and embarrassed England.

Attempts to counter the law breakers culminated in the passing in 1805 of a Bill that extended the Law Against Smuggling to 100 leagues from the mainland and embraced for the first time the Channel Islands. Relying on the Crown for protection in time of war, the Royal Court of Guernsey had little option but to accept it. This Act and the return to peace in 1815 curbed the trade, and the later reductions in import duties cut away the ground from smuggling generally.

Guernsey historians seem reluctant to admit the involvement of their compatriots. They sharply differentiate between the supply of goods afterwards smuggled and the act of smuggling itself. They appear to understate the island's complicity in the Trade, and to emphasise the good work that was undoubtedly done for the English by its privateers. Before 1815 (they said) Guernsey had limited shipbuilding facilities of its own and when war broke out the island bought vessels formerly employed as smugglers and fitted them out as privateers. But it is equally true that Guernsey bought such vessels in peace-time, though (one assumes) not for privateering. In the seven peace years preceding the war of 1793 the Port of Fowey transferred to Guernsey vessels at no less a rate than in the subsequent ten war years.

Generally speaking, the owners and masters of the Fowey vessels seized for smuggling belonged to the St. Austell/Fowey area, and as I found that the relevant ship registers at St. Peter Port were destroyed by enemy action it was not possible to ascertain what happened to Guernsey-registered craft. On the whole, the Guernseymen certainly kept out of the actual carriage of the goods and left this — subordinate — function to the mainlanders. Even so, Guernsey names among owners and masters of Fowey ships included: Ley, Allez, Nastell, Colinette, le Quesne, Leray, Vibert, Maujer, le Cronier; and even among ships seized and condemned were ones as prominent as 'le Mesurier'

17

and 'de Putron'. Carteret Priaulx himself was part-owner of the 75-ton Fowey sloop *New Fortune* (1789) seized soon after registration, as well as of Guernsey vessels.

While in the West Country smuggling carried little more shame with it than exceeding the speed limit does today (and was indeed praised in war-time even in the House of Lords), the Guernseymen also considered (certainly until the Act of 1805) that theirs was a time-honoured right not only to supply the smugglers but to collaborate with them. They retained mainland agents to market their goods, to collect their accounts, to keep them posted and to organise and protect the smugglers. Brokers specialised in providing finance for the Trade, and attorneys-at-law in winning minimal sentences for those brought to justice.

THE BANKS FAMILY

Prominent among Carteret Priaulx's agents was Lawrence (or Laurence) Banks, who traded with them as a principal. One who appears to be the same man was co-owner of the Fowey sloops *Brothers, Saint Michael* (1786) and the *Eagle* (1790). In 1786 he is described in the registers as a mariner of St. Austell and is shown as master of the *Brothers*. By 1790 he is described as a gentleman of St. Austell. Later his address moved to London, to Long Lane, Southwark, where he acted as Carteret's agent at least until July 1805, responsible, among other things, for the market in Wales which he visited frequently.

Lawrence Banks is not named in the Fowey registers later than 1790, and one might conclude that on moving to the capital he relinquished the St. Austell end of the business to others of his large family. At the time the names of seven other Banks do appear and there were other relatives engaged with him as well. Only one of these seven Banks did not reside in the St. Austell area, David Banks of Stoke Damerell, near Plymouth Dock, Gentleman, with interests in five vessels in 1786 and 1787, in all of which he was associated with other members of the family.

Another David Banks, clearly younger, is first recorded as a St. Austell mariner in 1789. In 1802 he owned and was master of the *Rashleigh*, built that year at Stonehouse, a 23-ton cutter, seized 1804 and sold to Falmouth. David is later shown as of Plymouth Dock, and in 1816 as a Stonehouse ship-builder. Two years later he went bankrupt, but the family business that he

so founded went on to build ships at Plymouth for a century.

From the number of vessels in which they held shares, the key members of the family after perhaps Lawrence were Kennett and William Banks. Kennett is described progressively as a St. Austell mariner, later as a victualler and later still as a gentleman, with shares in a dozen or so sloops and cutters. Of these at least three — the *Phoenix, Vigilance* and *Nancy* — were seized for smuggling. Then there was William Banks, mariner at first of St. Austell and later of Bristol. He too was part-owner or master of ships having Guernsey connections.

Two other Banks — Baker and Robert — were mariners, while William P. was a St. Austell cooper. The family was also concerned in the *Neptune*, a 111-ton brigantine built at Mevagissey in 1802, wrecked off St. John's, Newfoundland in 1818.

In the Carteret Priaulx papers Lawrence Banks refers several times to ships commanded by his nephews and, putting two and two together, it is hard to resist the conclusion that the family at St. Austell under his guidance and with his connections prospered in an organisation that ran contraband to a large part of the country. Of course, one cannot be certain of the relationships or that there was not more than one Banks at the same time and place with the same Christian name. But that the name 'Banks' was a power in the port of Fowey at the time is certain.

Banks sent frequent reports to his principals, preserved in their papers. For example, when in February 1804 he accompanied Captain Phillips to Westminster Hall for the trial of his cutter *Fly*, he reported that, though Phillips sat beside his counsel as bold as brass, the witnesses 'all swore she was within five leagues of the land'. The cargo was forfeited but the vessel was returned to its owners, a compromise that Banks considered was in their favour. He also reported that Carteret Priaulx's rival, Peter Maingy, was in Court at the same time and suffered the reverse decision — it was his cargo that was returned and his ship that was confiscated.

In a later report of 1804 from Caernarvon Banks gives the facts about the chase of a smuggler that was very likely the 107-ton cutter *Lion*, built at Mevagissey in 1798 and transferred from Fowey to Guernsey. Her master was John Phillips, and one of that name was one of Carteret Priaulx's principal captains. The *Lion* met up with the 16-gun Revenue Cruiser *Speedwell* of Milford, and the ensuing pursuit up and down the Welsh coast was the climax of Carteret Priaulx's long conflict with the Revenue. The chase went on for eleven days — but with what result was not disclosed!

The hazards run by the smugglers and their associates were not only from the Revenue, the elements and the enemy. Banks' correspondence shows that there were other dangers less dramatic. They embraced all those common to commerce, including default by debtors and saturation of markets. In addition the agent had to guard against dirty trickery by competitors that included use of informers, kegs of misleading size and robbery.

In the few years prior to the passing and enforcement of the 1805 Act these difficulties became exacerbated by the awareness of those concerned that the Trade was reaching its limits and that the need to reduce stocks and get money in was urgent. That it was boosted to its peak about 1805 finds confirmation in the graph below.

Carteret Priaulx in 1804 threatened Banks that he would give his North Wales business to James Randle, Jnr., of Cadgwith. 'There is no room for your Captain friend on this coast...' Banks wrote him when he heard. 'I already spend £400 a year to keep things as quiet as possible and even so the officers are very busy and take a quantity each trip...Your Captains and men can say I fag as much as possible and always pay them; they will inform you they would sooner take cargo for this coast than the north of Cornwall'.

The Guernsey firm did send their goods for North Wales through another agent but Banks wrote from Lampeter that 'none of the dealers worth trusting will take a cask from him...the greater part is in the storehouse'. And again 'had I known this vessel would land here I should have ordered my goods from Maingy & Brother...Pray say whether you mean to encourage Worrel & Co here and if so I shall candidly deal elsewhere. I do not deal with one man to pay the other nor never did'.

Carteret Priaulx himself, on one of his visits to his agents in Cornwall in 1805 wrote from Polperro in April: 'Pitt's infernal bill will, I fear, pass much too soon

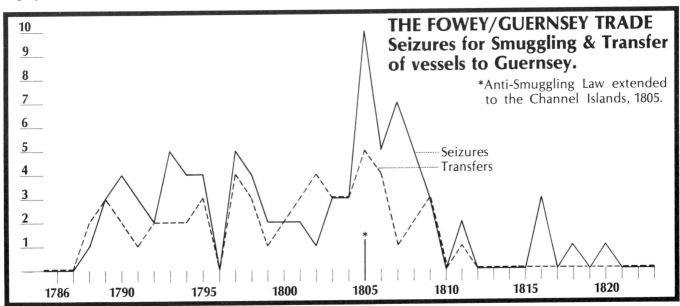

THE FOWEY/GUERNSEY TRADE
Seizures for Smuggling & Transfer of vessels to Guernsey.

*Anti-Smuggling Law extended to the Channel Islands, 1805.

Seizures
Transfers

13 GRAPH The Fowey/Guernsey Trade: Seizures for Smuggling & Transfers of Vessels to Guernsey 1786—1823.

The year is that of seizure or transfer. Where there is no record on the register of seizure date, the year six months after the last entry has normally been assumed to be that of seizure.

After 1820 only one seizure was recorded on the register (1835) and transfers to Guernsey were almost nil.

for us. If Hide and May, Hutton and Phillips could only make two or three voyages more they would reduce a little of our stock'. Payments due to his firm from Cornwall were in a state of disorder. 'I have been two days at Guerans and for eight hours did not quit my books putting Cregoe's accounts in order' — Thomas Cregoe of Gerrans, described as a fisherman, owned shares in Fowey vessels. — And again: 'This is a damn business for those who think and reflect; to ship and send account is nothing, to collect is the difficulty and at my age to be from my family is very unpleasant when a few years must carry me to my grave. I'm glad we shall not be long troubled with this damned business'.

MAINGY — AND OTHERS

The firm of Maingy & Brother was smaller than Carteret Priaulx & Co. They too had close connections with Fowey ships, combining the functions of merchants, ship-owners and mariners, with extensive vaults at St. Peter Port.

Nicholas and Thomas Maingy were based in Guernsey, while Peter Maingy tended the mainland from St. Austell and Stonehouse, Plymouth. Among other vessels they owned the *Swift*, built and registered at Fowey in 1799, a 162-ton cutter with 18 ports. In 1802 she was altered to a brigantine with a Time figurehead and, after being captured by the French but then re-taken, was registered at Guernsey in 1803. Her master was James Colinette, an island name.

Peter Maingy, described as a gentleman of St. Austell, owned the *Fly* (1797), a 79-ton shallop, rowing twenty oars and with stanchions for 12 swivel guns. She was seized and carried into Plymouth soon after registration. Her master's name was Daniel du Putron. Also the Maingys in 1803 bought out all their co-owners in the 100-ton cutter *Rose* (1799), built by John Allen of Mevagissey. She too was seized and broken up at Barnstaple in 1809.

Another family engaged in the Guernsey trade as owners, shipmasters and shipwrights were the Dunns of Mevagissey, who derived from Captain John Dunn, born 1726. The eldest of his eleven children was James who had close connections with Guernsey. He built, owned or had shares in Fowey cutters, sloops and luggers of which he or his relatives were masters. A portrait of James hangs in the little museum at Mevagissey.

James Dunn's sloops *Hope* and *Fortune* (1786), also the *Lord Nelson* (1800), were transferred to Guernsey, and among others that he owned or shared in were the following sloops, all seized for smuggling: *Venus* (1788) 87 tons; *Garland* (1791) 24 tons, ripped up in 1795; the *Clausina* (1794) 72 tons, seized 1805; and the *Fly* (1801) 40 tons. Two other of James' vessels were seized, both called the *Flora*: one a 53-ton sloop skippered by his brother Matthew and taken soon after being launched at Mevagissey in 1790; the other a 107-ton cutter built at Fowey in 1801 and seized five years later. James appears to have built, owned and captained her himself. Brother Matthew was also master of the *Reward* (1787). He lost his life when his ship capsized on the Handeeps off the Eddystone.

Another Dunn, Josiah, was owner and master of the 3-masted lugger *Lottery*, built (possibly by James) in the spring of 1805, 59 tons. She was registered on May 20 yet, on returning from Guernsey where her command was taken over by one John Dillon, she was seized on June 4 with contraband two leagues NNW of Padstow by the Revenue Cruiser *Shark*. Used temporarily as a revenuer from February to September 1806, she was broken up at Barnstaple in March 1807. Her 'lines' (*illustrated*) were taken and preserved at Hilhouse's Yard, Bristol. She should not be confused with another more notorious smuggler of the same name, a Polperro (Port of Looe) cutter, seized May 14 1799 by the Revenue Cruiser *Hinde*, Captain Gabriel Bray. Her story was told by Dr. Johnathan Couch in his *History of Polperro* but appears more reliably in the *Naval Chronicle*, May 18 1799 et seq.

The Dunn family became connected by marriage with the Leleans — a name possibly of Guernsey origin. Around the year 1800 five Leleans were masters of Fowey vessels, some of which were seized. James Dunn and the Leleans owned the 115-ton brigantine *Seven Brothers*, a prize taken from the French in 1800. Six years later the French took her back. Nicholas Lelean was her master.

Other families with whom the Dunns were connected by marriage included the Allens, also of Mevagissey, mariners and ship-builders. Dunn and Allen were agents at Coverack for Carteret Priaulx & Co. James Allen had shares in and skippered the sloop *Favourite* (1789). One of his sons took Holy Orders. John Allen was co-owner with Walter Cross of Mevagissey in the

22-ton sloop *Nancy* (1787). Cross was a smuggler. In 1796 he established the first stage-coach from Truro to Torpoint. John Allen, having lost his *Nancy* in 1789, became master of the 33-ton *Vigilance* the following year, alternating with Christopher Parnall of St. Austell. She was seized for smuggling. In 1802 he is shown as master of James Dunn's 57-ton lugger *Mary*.

Such families and relationships were typical of Fowey shipping and of the Trade. I would not wish to infer that they were considered by their peers as anything but respectable. The Dunns, mariners, fishermen and shipwrights who then numbered at least two clergymen in the family, owned or had shares in local vessels right through the 19th century. Notable members of recent generations have been and are well-known Trinity House pilots.

Christopher Parnall (or Parnell) was a prominent local smuggler of the time. He had interests in many vessels, varying upwards from 30 tons, mainly sloops or cutters, mostly Mevagissey-built. He, too, in the earliest registers is described as a mariner, and in the later ones as a gentleman, assisted thereto by his earnings from the Trade. To Guernsey, Parnall sold the sloops *Speedwell* (1795) 149 tons, and the *Hero* (1793) 90 tons, also the cutter *Speculator* (1800). He also owned the *Hawk* (1796) 70 tons, the *Abeona* (1790) 101 tons and the *Pomona* (1793) 43 tons — all seized and ripped up or sold.

Parnall appears to have been associated with Peter Maingy and with Zephaniah Job of Polperro, with whom he owned the *Lively* (1792), a 111-ton sloop transferred to Guernsey. Job was born at St. Agnes, Cornwall, and schooled to be a mine captain, an occupation requiring some training in figures. As a young man he got into a scrape and had to leave home. To earn a living he opened a school at Polperro but, lacking pupils, provided 'advice' to less educated people. He was appointed to keep the acounts of a privateer, through which he received £500 in prize money. With it he financed a business. He became accountant to East Cornwall smugglers and agent for the Guernsey merchants. But I found his name only twice among Fowey ship-owners — in the *Experiment*, 89-ton sloop of 1786, and the previously mentioned *Lively*.

Zephaniah backed others who did the smuggling. In time he became Polperro's Lord of the Manor, established his own note-issuing bank, owned the fee-simple of harbours and quays, brought the place into daily postal communication with Liskeard, and left a tidy fortune.

After about 1807 Fowey smuggling seizures became the exception and transfers of vessels to Guernsey suffered the same eclipse. By 1815 the Trade had faded. But it left its mark on local family fortunes. Cornishmen are still sometimes known by the soubriquet *Cousin Jack*, the euphemism by which the smugglers' cognac was once familiarly known.

14 Polperro.

CHAPTER TWO
LONGER VOYAGES, HEAVIER CARGOES, STRONGER SHIPS 1816–1840

No sudden change in the character of the port's ships occurred with the ending of the wars with France. The beginnings of change had already appeared between Trafalgar and Waterloo. They presaged a period of adjustment from which the maritime population of the area could hardly have benefited at the time.

Where between 1786 and 1815 an average of about 15 vessels had been registered in the port each year, the number more than halved in the subsequent twenty-five years; and the average tonnage remained much the same, around 68 (Appendix 'B'). As the ships were almost entirely locally owned, this indicates a major contraction in ship investment by the port's communities. Almost certainly this was because the tempting profits made from the Guernsey trade — hit hard by the Anti-Smuggling Act of 1805 — were no longer on offer. The decline in the number of seizures for smuggling after about 1807, and in the number of vessels transferred to Guernsey, both falling to near vanishing point by the late 1820s, support this view.

After 1815 the coasts either side of the Channel were closed to smuggling craft and, though the more determined offenders continued trading unlawfully for a good many years, drawing their supplies from Roscoff (to the warehouses of which Guernsey supplied the necessary casks, in the making of which its coopers were specially experienced), the scale was of a different order from what it had been. The risks to be run were much greater.

At the war's end over a quarter of a million fighting men were released to find employment that was only occasionally available. Some emigrated, those from Cornwall the forerunners of many who were to leave their homes fifty years later. In 1818 the '70-ton *Charlestown*, Williams master' was reported in the *West Briton* as sailing from Charlestown with fifty passengers for America, 'amongst whom are some whole families, including infants at the breast'.

This report of May 22 1818 has sometimes been taken to mean that the vessel herself sailed to America. Although there were emigrant craft of this size it is unlikely that she crossed the Atlantic. She was the sloop-rigged lighter already referred to, owned and

15 Coastguard watch-house at Polruan, c. 1860, one of a series around the coast.

22

commanded at the time by Richard Williams, a St. Austell mariner. She probably carried her passengers to Plymouth whence they transferred to another vessel. Upwards of 150 emigrants were reported in June 1818 as being about to embark at Plymouth. The passage to Canada cost five to six guineas; to the United States £7 (without provisions) or £11 (if provisions had to be supplied by the ship). Children went half price.

The threat to the Revenue of unemployed seamen swelling the smugglers' ranks was anticipated by the authorities who acted in various ways to strengthen the forces of prevention. In 1816 Revenue vessels were handed over to the Admiralty, no longer occupied by war. The following year a Coast Blockade was established. In 1822 the Coast Guard was brought into being. The number of preventive vessels was increased. At Fowey were stationed the Revenue Cruisers *Fox* and *Lion* (the agent for provisioning them was William Hicks, a Polruan butcher).

It is hardly surprising, then, to find that not only did the number and total tonnage of vessels decline, the proportion of sloops and cutters — the craft most suited to smuggling — fell sharply. Where in the earlier period they represented some 62% of ships registered, they accounted for only 43% between 1816 and 1840, and thereafter were to fall to a proportion of the whole that was negligible.

FROM CLINKER TO CARVEL

Another significant trend is revealed by analysis of the registers. From 1792 each vessel's type of construction was usually recorded and between that year and 1809, of vessels built and registered in the port, nearly twice as many were clinker than carvel. But from 1810 to 1830, with the exception of three vessels only (in 1816 and 1817), clinker building ceased. There was no co-relation between construction and size, rig or builder. Prior to 1810 many of the smallest craft were carvel, many of the largest clinker.

Why, then, this change? Might the timber famine have been a cause? Hardly, as to get the largest vessel out of a given timber supply could call for clinker building, as the planking could be thinner, strength being provided by the overlap. Might the cost of copper, which rapidly doubled by 1807, have had something to do with it? No, a carvel-built craft would not require less metal than one clinker-built and, in any case,

16 A Coastguard Sentry, 1831.

builders at that time were almost certainly relying on iron fastenings and trenails, not copper.

The answer is probably in the kind of cargoes carried. The Fowey builders had specialised in suiting the smugglers with craft that were economic, fast and manoeuvrable for cargoes relatively light in weight that called for no stronger construction than the cheapest. Of the 29 Fowey-built sloops and cutters recorded as being seized for smuggling between 1796 and 1807 only one was carvel built. And of *all* Fowey vessels seized more than twice as many were clinker than carvel.

It was particularly against the clinker-built cutter, with its retractable bowsprit and great spread of fore-and-aft canvas, that anti-smuggling legislation had been directed. For example, from 1784 no clinker-built vessels of any description were allowed unless they were square-rigged or sloops with standing bowsprits; any such, found in any port in the kingdom or within four leagues of the coast were liable to seizure. Hence such descriptions as 'cutter, clinker built, fitted as a sloop with standing bowsprit and legal stay'. Nevertheless, others that appear to have ignored the law were not uncommon, described on the register as (for example) 'cutter, clinker built with 18 ports' or 'cutter with 14 ports clinker built and running bowsprit'. It seems that it was one thing to pass laws, another to enforce them.

But after the 1805 Act extended the anti-smuggling laws to 100 leagues off the coast, thereby including the Channel Islands, it soon became apparent that the Guernsey trade was dying and that its clinker-built craft were back numbers. They were hardly capable of standing up to such as stone, coal and ore, or of being beached with any but light cargoes. These vessels were mostly cutters and after 1818 none were built.

Between 1796 (when the registers are sufficiently detailed) and 1836 (when methods of measuring tonnage were changed) some 71 craft described as cutters, averaging 78 tons, were built and registered in the port, and 94 sloops (see following table).

CUTTERS & SLOOPS BUILT & REGISTERED IN THE PORT OF FOWEY 1796—1836*

	Total No.	Average Tons (Old)	Carvel	Clinker	Unrecorded	Largest Carvel	Largest Clinker	Smuggling Trade		Transferred to other ports	Lost
								Seized, Rip'd Up.	Transferred to Guernsey		
CUTTERS	71 (a)	78 tons	7	61 (b) (e)	3	66 tons	167 tons	20 (c)	19	22	10 (d)
SLOOPS	94	54 tons	73 (k)	12 (f)	9	87	106 (1797)	9 (g)	5 (h)	43 (i)	23 (j)

(a) None after 1818   (b) 25 over 100 tons
(c) At least 16 between 1802 and 1809
(d) At least 7 between 1805 and 1809, all clinker
(e) 3 of 120—167 tons altered to brigs
(f) None after 1798, 1 only over 100 tons
(g) All 1796—1809, 6 in 1790s   (h) The last in 1798
(i) 19 with running bowsprits to ports west of Fowey
(j) At least 3 between 1805 and 1809
(k) 8 built 1809—1819; altered to 'Sloop' from 'Lighter' 1821—25; 4 altered to 'Schooner'.
   *The 1786—96 registries are too little detailed to warrant analysis.

Although both kinds of craft were involved in the Guernsey trade, the sloops were more commonly employed for heavier cargoes, mineral ore to South Wales, china clay to the Potteries, building stone, coal etc. It may be significant that of the 10 cutters lost at sea 1796—1836, 7 were lost between 1805 and 1809, all clinker-built, perhaps the result of their carrying heavier cargoes than was prudent.

In short, as smuggling declined, cargo-carrying increased, requiring heavier and thicker planking and carvel construction. On this the yards apparently concentrated all their production, even the smaller craft — a simplification of practice that could have had the effect of increasing productivity and lowering costs at a time when costs generally were rocketing.

THE SCHOONER RIG
Another change in the character of the ships also had its beginnings between Trafalgar and Waterloo, firmly establishing the schooner rig by the 1830s.

Fore-and-aft and sometimes with square topsails, it had migrated from Europe to the American colonies. There it was found particularly suitable for coasting and running to the West Indies and, in the earlier years of the 18th century it greatly increased in numbers. Many, if not most, of the colonial schooners were British built but with the establishment of their own yards the Americans constructed their own vessels. In the West Indies especially the schooner came to be used with foremast raking forward and mainmast raking aft, the *ballahou*.

The Americans made their own models sharper and faster. At the War of Independence, they were employing the rig on much larger vessels than were used in Europe, and by 1800 West country seamen frequenting the West Indies were fully familiar with the rig's advantages, especially after 1806 when the Cornish sought markets there for their pilchards to replace the big one in the Mediterranean cut off by Napoleon's blockade. In Jamaica alone, there were three million slaves on the plantations who had to be fed. It was from the West Indies that Swansea adopted the rig for its pilot vessels.

The first vessel at Fowey described as a schooner on her register was the *Mary* of May 17 1790, built at Mevagissey by Thomas Shepheard, 34 tons, 43 feet long. In 1793 there came the little 13-ton *Harriot*, built at Shelburne, Nova Scotia 1788. Another was built on

Fowey harbour in 1794 by John Wilcock, the *Friends' Endeavour* of 26 tons; and three prizes that were schooner-rigged were bought by local people 1801—2. With clinker-built cutters obsolete, the carvel-built sloops were barely suitable for trading to the distant parts now more necessary and made possible with safer seas. The schooners began slowly to increase in number and size after about 1807. The first of over 100 tons came from Nickels' yard as early as 1805. The *Alexander*, 107 tons, a brave innovation but not a success. She was lost in 1807. And the next of such size did not come off the slips till 1812; but by 1820 locally built 60-foot schooners of about 100 tons were not at all unusual.

The schooners were much easier to handle than the cutters when built to large dimensions (cutters went to 170 tons at Fowey), and they required fewer crew than square riggers of comparable size. Unlike the Americans, they retained their square topsails, which were more necessary in winds that were more variable than off the American coasts. But at first they failed to achieve as good speeds because the rig was used on hulls little different from those of the cutters and sloops. With experience they were gradually sharpened, and with the increase in deep-water trading the schooner, by 1830 or so, was on its way to becoming the rig most closely identified with Fowey.

The registers do not record voyages made but here and there are revealing indications — ports where masters were relieved, places where vessels were lost. Prior to the late 1820s there is little evidence of deep-sea trading but from 1829 an entry occurs with increasing frequency in connection with schooners especially: 'Mediterannean pass annexed to certificate of registry'.

Cornwall regained its main pilchard market, Italy, after the war and enormous supplies of casked, salted pilchards were shipped to the Mediterannean, an area that remained dangerous to shipping despite Viscount Exmouth's bombardment of Algiers in 1816 and the freeing of the Christian slaves on the Barbary Coast.

It was not until the capture of Algiers in 1830 by the French that ships trading to the Mediterannean became safe from attack by corsairs. Even then, for some years, an order in Council of 1819 specifically required them to carry their Mediterannean pass (instituted in 1722) attached to their certificate of registry, to confirm to the Algerians that British ships were under His Britannic Majesty's protection and, before ship registers were invented, were really British.

GROWTH OF SEA-BORNE HOME TRADE

Until Isambard Kingdom Brunel built his Royal Albert Bridge at Saltash in 1859, the last link in the railroad from Penzance to Paddington, the sea was the highway from Cornwall to London, between which most goods went coastwise.

In 1824 a regular service was provided by the lengthily titled Fowey, Bodmin, Lostwithiel, St. Austell and Mevagissey Shipping Company. It was a joint venture by two London wharfingers and a number of Fowey and St. Austell merchants and grocers who owned the three 'strongly built' schooners comprising the company's fleet. They were: the *Ann & Elizabeth*, Jacob Moyse master, 87 tons, built in 1818 and owned by the Moyse family and Thomas Breeds and Thomas Farncombe of Griffin's Wharf, Southwark; the *Fowey*, Moses Bone master, 101 tons, built 1812, owned by various local traders; and the *Charles Rashleigh*, John Pearce master, 73 tons, built 1824 and owned by James Burnett, Fowey merchant and 21 others.

An advertisement of March 11 1824 said the vessels would load at Griffin's Wharf but that none 'will remain longer at the wharf than 18 days'. They would 'regularly follow each other'. The venture does not appear to have lasted very long. Between 1831 and 1834 the three schooners were sold.

Traffic between the Cornish mines and the smelters of South Wales was all sea-borne. Until 1836 every block of tin went by sea, and china clay and stone to the Severn and Mersey for the Staffordshire Potteries all had to be shipped into the Atlantic swell and cross seas around Land's End.

Various means of avoiding the hazards of this route were considered. Borlase, the Cornish historian, had suggested a canal to connect the Fowey and Camel rivers, and a number of possibilities were investigated in the 1790s without result. In 1825 Marc Isambard Brunel planned a route for a 13-mile ship canal linking Fowey harbour with Padstow on the north Cornish coast but it proved too costly, especially with the new power of steam in prospect.

Meanwhile, major improvements and extensions were in train within the limits of the port itself. In 1826 an artificial harbour was built at Pentewan to provide an

17 Charlestown about 1904, showing entrance to the basin cut from solid rock more than a century previously when Charles Rashleigh built the harbour for St. Austell, prior to which cargoes were shipped to and from beaches.

National Maritime Museum

outlet more accessible than Charlestown to St. Austell with which it was linked by rail to carry the china clay to ship-side. In 1830 Joseph Thomas Austen (1782—1850), a mining 'adventurer' of enterprise and energy, fulfilled a long projected plan originally intended for the export of his granite and copper ore; he built an artificial tidal harbour at Par on a large area recovered from the sea. To it he added a smelter for producing silver from galena lead, brick works, a pilchard fishery, a ship-building yard, sail loft, a granite cutting and dressing yard and, for the mines, a candle factory. He thus founded what became a thriving maritime community of mariners, shipowners, craftsmen and merchants that complemented the mining population in the neighbourhood. In 1836 he became Sheriff of Cornwall and assumed the name and arms of Treffry of Place, Fowey.

Another improvement was of a different order. The bold Gribben headland, which bounded St. Austell Bay to the east, was easily mistaken for other promontories, especially the Dodman and St. Anthony's Head at the entrance to Falmouth. Three losses in December 1830 caused Trinity House to erect on it in 1832, a distinguishing beacon tower, 84 feet tall and 250 feet above sea level, painted in distinctive red and white bands. It also served as a leading mark to Fowey harbour and a bearing to the newly-improved havens of Par, Pentewan and Mevagissey.

In 1838 Treffry acquired the little five-year-old fishery harbour at Newquay on the north Cornish coast, and proceeded to reconstruct and expand it into general trading, tapping by a mineral railway the output of mines to the west and china clay works to the south, thus avoiding the hazards of the Land's End passage. It became important for the shipment of iron ore and china clay and for the import of coals.

Newquay harbour was also a badly needed refuge for vessels navigating the Bristol Channel. For example, on the night of February 3 1843 the brigs *Juliana*, John Welsford, and *Erato*, William Shea, in difficulties in a NNW gale, discovered to their surprise the lights of the new and largely unknown harbour, ran for it and were saved by it from certain disaster. But by then, of course, the railways were revolutionising communications. Sea was no longer the only route for heavy goods up-country.

INDUSTRY, NOT SHIPS, ATTRACTS CAPITAL

It was the mines, quarries and clay works of the Fowey/St. Austell area that now almost wholly determined the shipping activity of its harbours and beaches. And it is surprising that in these post-war years they did not bring about the investment of more local money in shipping than they did. Even at that date a large proportion of the area's increasing industrial output must have been carried away in bottoms owned elsewhere.

Copper had become far more important than tin, and Cornwall now dominated the world copper ore markets. By 1805 the copper price had doubled in twenty years and by 1825 the output was twice what it had been forty years previously. The copper mines in the Charlestown/Fowey area were unprecedented successes. For Crinnis, the first of the rich copper mines in the locality, in four months in 1813 no less than 49 cargoes of ore were despatched from Charlestown harbour, a quantity of 3,792 tons limited only by available shipping space. Between 1831 and 1840 Cornish copper was to account for half world production.

18 'For the Safety of Commerce and for the Preservation of Mariners', this beacon, 84 ft high and 250 ft above sea level, was erected on the Gribben headland in 1832 by the Corporation of Trinity House of Deptford Strond to distinguish it from two other promontories, the Deadman (or Dodman) and St. Anthony's Head, Falmouth. It also served as a leading mark to Fowey Harbour, and a bearing to Par, Pentewan, Charlestown and Mevagissey.

Copper more than made up for declining tin output in the St. Austell area where, also, the tin quality was of the best, and the Welsh tinplate works (of which there were sixteen by 1825) would take nothing less.

In addition to five rich copper and tin mines that came into production in the area by 1840, an iron mine close to Lostwithiel in the Fowey river valley was being worked by 1839.

Quarries were busy. Luxulyan granite had been used for the lighthouse and beacon on Plymouth's new breakwater, and Pentewan building stone was being shipped far afield. Much more important, the production of china clay and stone from the works

27

19 Two pages from account book of sloop *Sally* of 1808, kept by the owner John Climo.

around St. Austell by 1830 had grown steadily from 2,000 tons in 1800 to five and six times that figure.

All this activity and output during the 1816—1840 period might be expected to have brought with it an increase in the number of ships registered and in the tonnage of those built in local yards. It did not happen. Perhaps such risk capital as there was went into the mines and clay works. People had put money into smuggling vessels but were averse to shipping investment post-war.

Where in the twenty-five years 1790—1815 some 260 vessels were locally built and put on the register, in the same length of time ending 1840 the equivalent figure is only 132, ships of much the same average tonnage.

The probability is that, unless they came from the mines, the dividends of lawful business after the war were less tempting than those earned in the Guernsey trade.

A WAY OF LIFE

The surviving accounts of small merchantmen are few and far between for any period but they do exist for one little vessel 1820—1822 and suggest that most local ship-owning was a modest way of life rather than an attracter of capital. The sloop *Sally* was a typical Fowey coaster of the time by size, build and trade — 49 tons, carvel-built in 1807, running bowsprit, square stern, 48'6" x 16'3" x 7'10". She was owned by John Climo, her master one of a family of mariners experienced in managing vessels of the kind, and was normally employed for eleven months of the year carrying copper ore, limestone, corn, barley (Looe—Bristol), iron, culm (anthracite slack) and South Wales coals. She traded to and from all points between Plymouth and Newport.

To the nearest pound her profit was £7 in each of the three years 1820, 1821 and 1822. Climo himself took out £47 per annum in wages, and 'lived off' the *Sally* before arriving at his profit. Also while he normally acted as a carrier he always traded as a principal for culm and coals, from which he would have made a profit as a dealer.

So the *Sally* enabled her owner to make a living; to provide 'vittles' and pay for his three employees, probably relatives, and to carry on the business of coal supplier, whence most of his income probably came — an economic unit not greatly different from a small coal merchant-cum-carrier today with a couple of lorries. That it functioned satisfactorily despite or because of its small size seems to be borne out by the facts that the family added one or two other little vessels as the years passed, that the *Sally* lasted fifty eight years till she foundered on the Longships in 1865 on voyage from South Wales to Plymouth, and that Climos continued as village coal merchants until the 20th century.

TIMBER SHORTAGE AND COST

A factor that must have limited the ability of local shipyards to meet such demand as there was for schooners of larger size suitable for distant trading, was the shortage and high cost of timber, dating from the famine years around 1809.

Such timber as Cornwall ever grew had long been depleted by the use for tin smelting of vast quantities of charcoal, displaced by sea-coal. Though from time to time even into the 19th century there were in east Cornwall occasional sales of oak of ship-building quality, the Navy's appetite for timber was insatiable. To build an average 74-gun ship-of-war had required the equivalent of stripping sixty acres of century-old oaks.

The resultant crippling scarcity had worsened in 1807 when the anti-British blockade had cut off supplies from the Baltic. Behind the continuing shelter of a duty on Baltic timber, Canadian supplies had been brought in, laying the foundations of the trans-Atlantic timber trade, and these led to softwood ships themselves being bought from yards in Prince Edward Island, Nova Scotia and New Brunswick, yards that had been established largely by West Country emigrants.

The first Canadian-built craft at Fowey was a little schooner called the *Harriot*, 13 tons, acquired by the ship-builder Nickels in 1793, but she was a *rara avis* without significance. It was in 1834 that local mariners and merchants began a trend that lasted for forty years by buying softwood schooners, brigs and barques from Canada that were larger than most Fowey-built craft of the time. The first three of these, bought in the 1830s, may well have helped local adjustment to the schooner rig on deep-water vessels; and builder, owner and mariner alike were now obliged to accept alternatives to English oak.

SHIPBUILDING CHANGES

These so-called 'Plantation built' ships represented a major threat of competition to the port's yards, especially as it was the larger owners whose interest was attracted by them mainly for deep-sea employment. They probably had an enlivening effect.

While from the registers it is possible to arrive at a rough idea of builders' relative outputs, the figures are necessarily incomplete and approximate, but they do confirm what might otherwise have been envisaged — that in the post-war period the output of the Mevagissey yards fell while those on Fowey harbour grew. (Appendix 'E').

At varying times in the 1786—1815 period, specialising in the smuggling cutters and sloops for which they were well known, there were seven builders on Mevagissey Bay. They turned out at least 110 ships that went on the Fowey register, averaging around 78 tons apiece. But between 1816 and 1840 only three builders seem to have worked there — that is, builders of craft of over 15 tons. In Mevagissey these were Nicholas Lelean from 1823 to 1874, and Peter Smith until about 1820 only; also at nearby Portmellon James Dunn succeeded by Walter Dunn about 1834. To them I can attribute only 25 ships in the period, averaging about 80 tons.

Where in the 'Free trade' years to 1815 the Mevagissey yards were building an average of at least 284 tons per year this tonnage dropped to 80 in the subsequent twenty-five years — a collapse of more than two-thirds, almost certainly caused by the loss of the Guernsey trade.

After Waterloo, building began at Charlestown on St. Austell Bay, which added to that of Mevagissey and meant that between 1816 and 1840 the total of ships turned out in that part of the port west of the Gribben was 35 ships, averaging 77 tons.

East of the Gribben on both banks of Fowey harbour, five yards, 1786—1815, built at least 49 ships averaging 70 tons, whereas in the ensuing twenty-five years their output grew to 72 vessels of much the same size. While the Fowey yards built vessels that came to be used for smuggling, the extent of their reliance on them seems to have been less than at Mevagissey, neither was such

a high proportion of their output transferred to Guernsey.

The principal builders in Fowey were Thomas Nickels, succeeded by his son George: and William Brokenshaw. On the west bank, their yards were on the south side of Caffa Mill Pill, a substantial creek today infilled to serve as a car and boat park, and at nearby Pottery Corner.

I have already referred to both Nickels' and will not do so again. William Brokenshaw, a contemporary, was not so productive, working between 1813 and 1857. He built at least 18 Fowey-registered ships over that time and smaller craft probably as well. Two-thirds of them were schooners, several employed in the codfish trade

20 Bodinnick Ferry, steel engraving after Thomas Allom (from *Cornwall Illustrated 1831*). In the distance is Caffa Mill Pill where shipyards were occupied successively by Nickels, Brokenshaw, Heller and possibly others. Today, infilled, it is a car and boat park. Foreground left of the scene was described in 1838 as 'Shipwright's yard, house and garden' owned by Lady Grenville and occupied by John Marks, shipwright, who built vessels 1826—1846, succeeded in 1868 as occupant by Nicholas and Joseph Butson.

from Newfoundland to the Mediterannean. In 1837 he launched a 51-ton sloop called the *Standard* for Joseph Thomas Treffry. She was in service until 1917, a life of 80 years. In the 1840s Brokenshaw seems to have occupied part of Nickels' yard.

On the easterly and more sheltered bank of the harbour, in the parish of Lanteglos-by-Fowey, William Geach and Son, Polruan, whom I have already mentioned briefly, traded till about 1840, launching at least 20 vessels of 15 tons and over, mainly sloops and smacks. They were a family of boatwrights, shipwrights, mariners and house builders. In 1836 or early 1837 they went bankrupt, Captain James Geach dying about the same time, leaving a number of houses he was building uncompleted. Whatever the circumstances, in 1840 the Geach property was auctioned, including 17 houses mostly built by Captain Geach.

Their shipwrights' yard, at the extremity of Polruan near the entrance to Fowey harbour, possessed 'every accommodation for building and launching vessels of large burthen, having upwards of 16 feet of water at spring tides'. It had store houses, moulding loft, two uncompleted dwelling houses and an excellent well of water. At the time of the sale the yard was let to Messrs. Marks & Rendle.

John Marks and William Rendle first appear as Fowey shipwrights in 1825 when they bought shares in a ten-year-old schooner, *Duke of Wellington*. Probably brothers-in-law, they came from Polperro and adjacent Talland where there was a large family of Rendles, coopers, mariners, cordwainers and shipwrights. John Rendle, shipwright, who died in 1826, was sole owner of the 121-ton schooner *Two Brothers* that had been built in 1820 at Polperro, then part of the port of Looe, and it is likely that he was the builder of this and other vessels (for example, the sloop *Sisters* in 1822) at Talland Bay, much better suited to the purpose than Polperro's squeezed and crowded harbour. What is certain is that in 1826 John Marks, shipwright, signed the builder's certificate at Fowey for the 60-ton sloop *Abeona*, and by 1830 was partnered there by William Rendle. Over the next twenty years they turned out at least 22 sloops and schooners of up to 100 tons or so.

John Marks lived at Bodinnick (directly opposite Caffa Mill Pill on the Fowey side), occupying the shipyard which subsequently became 'Ferryside', the first Cornish home of the du Maurier family. It seems to have been insufficient for the building of what was more than one ship a year, hence their leasing as well Geach's yard in Polruan. While his partner lived at Bodinnick, Rendle lived at the Polruan yard; and it is almost certain that the five ships ascribed to him on their registers, built during the period of the lease, were turned out there in Polruan while the others came off Marks' slipway up the harbour.

Also living at Geach's yard in Polruan at the time they went bankrupt was Nicholas Butson, a shipwright who probably worked either for Geach or for Rendle or both. And, not only did Marks & Rendle step up their output to at least 7 vessels in four years, Butson made Geach's misfortune the occasion to go into business on his own account. And the first vessel attributed to him was the *Gallant* of 1839, a 110-ton schooner commissioned by Joseph Thomas Treffry.

AN INDUSTRIALIST'S FLEET

As I have already said, Treffry was one of the largest industrialists in Cornwall in the first half of the 19th century, a man of enterprise who had established mines, granite quarries, railways and other undertakings. As early as 1813 he had had a survey made of Fowey harbour which described it as 'better calculated than any other harbour in the west of England for wet and dry docks on a scale suitable for merchantmen'.

Between 1821 and 1847 he owned outright some 13 Fowey ships, with lesser interests in three others. He owned as well half-a-dozen or so barges and lighters. Some of these were lost or sold off but most were kept permanently employed in the work of his various undertakings. They included the snow *Susanna* of 1821 (for 5 years); the sloops *Hero* of 1820 (30 years), *Lucy* of 1820 (8 years), *Venus* of 1828 (9 years), *Model* of 1840 (10 years), *Hydra* of 1830 (16 years); and the schooners *Union* of 1820 (8 years), *Par* of 1836 (14 years), *Langurthowe* of 1837 (13 years), *Gallant* of 1839 (11 years) and *New Quay* of 1847 (4 years). His principal master mariners were the Climos (William, George and Sam), Thomas Scantlebury, Joseph Ellery, William Toms and John and Sam Dyer.

Most of his vessels had been built in the port, but with his developing interests in Newquay on the north coast he commissioned a schooner from Thomas Evans at Bideford — the *Par*. She was launched in the spring of

1836 and was followed by another from the same yard, the *Langurthowe*, completed a year later. Both were in the region of 86 tons. They were followed in 1839 by the schooner *Gallant* (110 new tons) and, a few months later, the sloop *Model* (60 new tons). But these two were built for him by Nicholas Butson, a Polruan shipwright who thereby became a master builder late in life, being about 60 years of age at the time.

OWNER—BUILDER RELATIONSHIPS — 1839

Among the Treffry family papers are Butson's accounts for the *Gallant* but, as he was responsible for the hull only, they do not reveal a certain total of all costs (summarised at Appendix 'I'). Sails, blocks, ropes, *etc.*, were supplied by other than Butson and paid for direct by Treffry's manager at Par, while Captain William Climo seems to have had charge of 'building work', perhaps bringing everything together.

Butson's charge for constructing the *Gallant*'s hull (141 'old' tons) — shipwrights', joiners', caulkers' and sawing work — adds up to £540 or £3.82 per ton. The work took eleven months. All the accounts as preserved, whether complete or not, total £972, and that may have been approaching the approximate aggregate cost (£6.89 per ton), excepting that an account for the spars seems to be missing, Butson's bill saying 'The cost of the spars you may git of Capn. Climo

if you have not gut it'. Ten years previously, by the way, Treffry had bought the new sloop *Venus* from her builder, John Hocking of Catdown, Plymouth, for £240 (£4.36 per ton).

Whatever the figures, Treffry's policy in equipping his undertakings with at least some of the cargo-carrying capacity they needed minimised any middleman's profit. No supplier took a profit from him for goods furnished by someone else. He bought direct.

When after completing the *Gallant* Butson came to quote Treffry for building 'a smack aboute 8ft 6ins deep to admeasure about 80 tons' — the *Model* — the wording of the agreement, written by Butson, exemplifies the relationship between the two parties. He agreed to do the shipwrighting and joiners' work on the vessel

'bellow the reails exclusive of all sawing, blockmaking, penting, cabening and spars. All timber to be drunken longside the pit and a boy to be provided from the yeard to go the arrunds, turn the stone and tend the killn like the(y) have at Bideford. All metearials with...to be provided by the yeard in the useal way. The labor part to be don fur 40/- per ton old measurment and four pounds fur laying down and making the moulds...The wadges to be paid as before and the accounts to be settled when the vefsell is fit fur sea'.

CHAPTER THREE
THE SCHOONERS AND THEIR BUILDERS 1841–1880

From 1841 the limits of the port were extended eastwards to the west bank of the Seaton River to take in Looe and Polperro. Looe (including Polperro) had been a port of registry in its own right from 1679 to 1832 but had then become absorbed into the port of Plymouth, its neighbour to the east. So it remained until 1841 when it was considered more appropriate to the port of Fowey, the main character of which as we know it today, in extent, capability and trade, was shaped in these middle years of the century.

It was then that locally-owned merchant sail reached its peak, trading mainly coastwise but also to the Mediterranean, Newfoundland, the West Indies and the Americas. It was then that steamships began to complement and rival sail, that china clay exceeded mineral ores as the principal outgoing cargo. It was then that, iron having superseded wood, local ship-building effectively ceased after a zenith in the Seventies, and the port's yards became occupied solely with repairing and with the building of craft for fishing and recreation.

However, in the Hungry Forties one preliminary to this was a resurgence of smuggling, with Roscoff as the entrepôt, though on nothing like the scale of sixty years earlier when the cognac run into Cornwall alone represented a yearly revenue loss equal to the

21 Connected with Liskeard by rail and part-way by canal, Looe shipped mineral ores, granite and pilchard, took in mainly coal, timber and grain. Here are three schooners about 1900 alongside Downgate Quay, East Looe, and the stores of Blamey & Morcom, Liskeard merchants. West Looe is opposite. Pre-1914 the railway wagons ran the length of Downgate Quay instead of stopping short at the bridge up-river as in later years.

estimated yield of the notorious Stamp Duties from the American colonies.

The last scrimmage of any account between Coastguards and smugglers on the Cornish coast had occurred in March 1834, when just east of Fowey a large body of men, making a landing of goods at Lantic Bay, were surprised by Coastguards and a detachment from the *Fox* cutter. Subsequently, although a reward was made for the seizure, no 'blood money' was paid as none of the accused charged at Bodmin were convicted.

The following year the 51-ton sloop *Jubilee*, Bideford built in 1809, was seized for smuggling and broken up at Padstow — the only recorded seizure of a Fowey vessel subsequent to 1820. Her owner was John Webb, a Mevagissey mariner who was also her master.

Commander H.N. Shore, in his *Smuggling Days & Smuggling Ways* (1892) says that by the 1840s the 'illicit trade' was now chiefly conducted in foreign bottoms but that English vessels *en route* from port to port took in contraband mid-Channel from others sent to meet them. Of the worst offenders in this line of business he names three of Fowey — the *Place*, the *Boconnoc* and the *One & All*. All three were registered at Fowey in 1836 in the ownership of Anthony Luke, a St. Austell cooper, and John Mills Carkeet, a Fowey merchant. They sold the sloop *Place* to Plymouth in 1840, but the others they had lengthened in 1838 to 51/52 feet and 37/38 tons, re-rigged as schooners and given Mediterranean passes. They sold them in 1845 and 1847 respectively.

It was Free Trade that all but wiped out the last of the 'Free Traders'. The first levy to go was the odious Salt Tax hated by the Cornish poor, then the restrictive Excise Duties. Tariffs were cut in 1842, 1845 and 1846 — 1,200 articles rapidly freed from duty. In 1849 the repeal of the Navigation laws opened British ports — and even the coasting trade — to foreign ships. By the late 1850s even the remnants of 'the Trade' belonged to the past.

Today the only visible signs of their one-time existence are the few little cliff-top watch-houses surviving from the chain erected to house 'flying detachments' of Coastguards in critical locations between the permanent stations. There is still one on Lantivet Bay halfway between Fowey and Polperro, and another (now used by the Trinity House pilots) on St. Saviour's Hill, Polruan. Both were built about 1863.

SHIPS' LONGEVITY

As at December 31 1850 there were 137 vessels on the register, getting on for three times as many as there were in 1792. Most of them — over 100 — have been built in the port's own yards. The average tonnage was much larger, 78 compared with 46, and this was reflected in the average size of the crew — five compared with four.

Of these vessels 38 were subsequently transferred to other ports but, as 99 remained on the Fowey register and the names of the ships appear on the registrar's 1850 list (see Appendix 'H') it is possible to ascertain their years of build and demise. The combined life of these 99 vessels was found to be 3,819 years, about 39 years each on average, which was also about the life of the 60 schooners. The sloops (22) and smacks (5) had the longest lives, 44 and 47 years respectively. The shortest lives were of the 2 barques (32 years) and a brig (10).

22 The Hon. Henry N. Shore RN when, a naval lieutenant, he was appointed Inspecting Officer of H.M. Coastguard, serving in England and Scotland 1881—1889, and began his study of 'smuggling days and ways'. Author and illustrator, he recorded the recollections of local old-timers at Fowey where he lived.

The Hon. Mrs. J. Barnwell

MID-CENTURY 'BOOM'

As stated, these figures are only of the vessels on the register as at December 31 1850 (12.00 midnight); but analysis of numbers, kinds and sizes of vessels registered from 1841 to 1880 inclusive shows that investment in local ships reached its peak in this 'boom' period. Also the owners' addresses show that well over 80% of the capital came from the St. Austell/Fowey/Liskeard area, south-east Cornwall, though shares tended to move elsewhere with the passing of time.

Between 1841 and 1880 (Appendix 'B') some 319 vessels were entered on the Fowey register, an average of 8 per annum, a figure little different from that between 1816 and 1840. But the average tonnage, at 110, was getting on for two-thirds greater than previously. Indeed, the figures, such as they are, show clearly that the size of the port's vessels gradually grew throughout the period; and this is also true of those built locally (Appendix 'D'), which averaged much the same tonnage as all those registered, which of course included others built elsewhere.

SCHOONERS 60%

The schooner was by far the commonest rig by this period during which the size of the schooners grew consistently. Where they averaged about 79 tons in the 1840s, they were 88 tons in the 1850s, 92 tons in the 1860s, and 116 tons in the 1870s. In feet, the average length grew from 62 — 68 — 75 — 87. The largest of these schooners was a 3-master of 1877, the *Natal*, 214 tons, built at Alloa on the Forth in 1861, bought from Plymouth owners by William Couch, master mariner of Bodmin and Par. She was lost at Dunkirk in 1897.

As many as 60% of ships that went on the register between 1841 and 1880 were schooners and only 8% were described as sloops and cutters — compared with the 1786—1815 picture, a complete reversal that had taken place over sixty or so years. Also what were described as brigantines were about 17% of the total where previously they were a good deal less.

But such figuring is approximate if only because rig nomenclature was still loose in definition. Although the word 'barquentine' was used from the late 17th century, I can find no vessel at Fowey so-called earlier than the 290-ton, *William Geake* of 1876, when, prior to her, there were at least eight vessels with three masts

apiece described as 'brigantine'. The *Platina* of 1853 is loosely called 'A square rigged vessel with three masts'. The 3-masted *Florence*, built at Looe by Henry Shapcott in 1869, is delightfully and uniquely described as a 'barquette' — a French word meaning 'skiff or small rowing boat' but here probably intended to convey the idea of a small barque. She was 198 tons.

OWNERS PER SHIP

Expectedly, increased size brought with it an expansion in the number of owners per ship at any one time and a contraction in the number of 64ths held by each. The greater the capital at risk the greater the need to spread it. Thus the schooner *Ann & Elizabeth*, built and registered at Fowey in 1830, had as many as 34 owners by August 1843. The Merchant Shipping Act of 1854, however, imposed a maximum per ship of 32 owners, so we find that when Robert Mark, a Liskeard gentleman, had it written in 1875 as having sold two of his four 64ths in the brigantine *Undine* to William Morgan of Aberdare, the transaction had to be expunged as invalid, the vessel already having 32 owners.

In those days ship-owning was very personal, each owner normally being at least on nodding terms with master and crew and often, indeed, related by family ties. It continued so to be long after the Companies Act (Limited Liability) of 1855 enabled family businesses to convert into joint stock companies, a change that only exceptionally affected ship-owning at Fowey and no earlier than towards the close of the century. Today the 32-owners limit has long been redundant though a restriction remains on the number who can hold 64ths jointly. The 32-owners limit was sometimes circumvented. When the *Ocean Spray* was registered on July 10 1877 she was, *de jure*, shown as having thirty owners; but when the ship's account book was opened, thirty-nine were named *de facto*.

'Shipowner' as a description of occupation appeared only rarely in the register prior to the 1860s, and then it became more frequent, perhaps made desirable by publicity given to Samuel Cunard, ship-owner, being elevated to a baronetcy by Her Majesty in 1859.

Though *Pigot's Directory* of the area has ten names under 'Shipowners' for 1823/4, these people were not described that way in the register but by the work they did — mariner, ship-builder, sailmaker, merchant, *etc.*, with two exceptions — 'Gentleman' and 'Esquire'.

'Shipowner' is hardly a description of occupation, any more than 'shareholder'. Of the many hundreds of owners of 64ths in local vessels it is doubtful whether the income of more than a handful was derived solely or even mainly from those investments. Justifiable by possession of as little as only one 64th, 'shipowner' nevertheless has a grand ring to it, sometimes misleading as to the affluence of forebears.

THE TADDS

Shipowning in a small port like Fowey can easily be seen to be very much of a family business right down to recent times, often having its genesis in a few 64ths held by the master of someone else's ship. Indeed, some families that 150 years ago were mariners and owners still exert an influence on the shipping of the place despite the de-personalisation of capital.

The small village of Polruan alone can furnish several dynastic examples. Until the present century it was dominated by a few seafaring families, a village where perhaps every other habitation was the shore home of one and sometimes several mariners. Perhaps the most notable were the Tadds and the Hockens.

The Tadds seem to have been earlier on the scene, embracing several generations of master mariners. Peter (d. 5.11.1832) first appears modestly in 1806 as co-owner and master of the barge *Providence*, then of a lighter of 1810, the *Ant*. But before he died he had interests in at least seven other vessels, often in company with Peter II (d. 1868), Thomas, John and William (d. 1868), vessels of which one or other was master.

By the 1850s there was also Peter III, James, Samuel (d. 1882), Thomas Werry (d. 1884), Jonathan Werry (d.1880) and John Werry — all described as master mariners with the exception of one shipwright and a victualler. In the 1860s there were probably eight or nine master mariner Tadds living in the village, all owners more or less, aside from other seafaring males of the family by marriage. Four Tadds were landowners in the parish by 1838.

In the 1840s six or more vessels of from 70—160 tons were being managed or commanded by one or other Tadd, and they were principally deep-sea general cargo traders. The most lasting investment seems to have been the 104-ton schooner *Bedwelty*, built for them in 1841 by John Tredwen of Padstow. Her masters were Samuel and James, and she ran frequently to the Mersey with china clay. Samuel and Jane Tadd had a son christened James Liberty born aboard her in 1852, after which Samuel is described as 'of Birkenhead'. The son emigrated to Canada.

The little *Isabella* of 1865, later owned by John Stephens, was managed to 1886 by the Tadds who employed her in coasting and occasionally to Newfoundland and the Mediterranean. With her they were more fortunate than with some others. Between 1838 and 1878 they lost seven out of fourteen ships. Perhaps the worst loss was of the 97-ton schooner *Emily Ellen*, launched for them by John Stribley at Padstow in 1872. She too traded to the Mediterranean and elsewhere but for five years only. She was presumed to have foundered on passage to Liverpool in March 1878 with all hands, including her master Peter Tadd III. After that the family acquired no other interest in Fowey vessels, with one exception, the barquentine *Lydia Cardell*; her managing owner from 1897 to 1903 was Elias Roskelly Tadd (1840—1908).

The last master mariner of this Polruan family was Captain Martyn Tadd (1872—1959). I have been told, but have no firm evidence of it, that one Tadd ship traded as distantly as the China Coast.

THE HOCKENS

The Hockens were contemporaneous with the Tadds. They had interests, albeit sometimes small, in some forty ships, including major holdings in twenty over the eighty years that ended with the wreck of the *Ada Peard* in 1916. In that time they lost only six or seven vessels, a fine record for a family that was as heavily engaged in the deep-sea trades as any other in the locality.

The ships they managed and commanded were bigger than the Tadds', especially after the 1870s. Fourteen of them were square-rigged, brigantine or barquentines, including the biggest, the *E.S. Hocken*, sold before she was lost in 1917. Three of the others were well over 250 tons: the *Ada Peard* (256) built by Samuel Moss at Par 1875; the *Ocean Ranger* (281) built at Appledore in the same year; and the *Ocean Spray* (267) also by Moss two years later. (See Appendix 'K').

'Mr. Hocken' is recorded in the parish tithe map as 'Officer of the Coast Guard' in 1838, but in the ship register Hockens first appear with John as master in 1830 of Joseph Thomas Austen's 55-ton sloop *Venus*. In 1836 John, Edward and William were part owners in a

				£
E. S. Hocken				
1880	Profits Divid⋅			1000
1881	Do	Do		768
1882	Do	Do		896
1883	Do	Do		320
1884	Do	Do		800
1886	Do	Do		384
1887	Do	Do	5248 5496	272
1888	Do	Do	2.48	160
1889	Do	Do		512
1890	Do	Do		384
				5496
	First Cost of the E.S. Hocken			5248
	Balance over first Cost =			248
1891	Profits Divid⋅ between the owners.			352
1892	Call made £5 per Share			
1893	Profits £3 per Share			192
94	" "	"		192
95	"	£3 -10 - "		224
96	"	1 -10 Remetalled		96
97	"	3 -10		224
Jan. 99	"	4 -10		288
Aug 1900	"	3 - 0 Remetalled		192
Sept 1901	"	6 - 10 (1905 Remetalled)		416
Oct 1907	"	2 - 0		128
April 1908	"	5 - 0 Remetalled		320
May 1909	"	3. 0		192
Oct 1910	"	1 -10 Retreenailed		96
May /11	"	3. 0		192
Oct /11	"	3. 0		192

23 Profits summary of the *E.S. Hocken*, 1880—1911, from her account book. She was the family's biggest vessel and paid for herself in her first ten years. The largest built in the port of Fowey, 296 tons, 126 feet long.

Ocean Ranger
List of owners & Amounts Paid

				£ s d
1	Revd Dr. Treffry	4 Shares.		£268 - -
2	William Leatherby.	8 "		536 - "
3	J. H. Hocken	4 "		268 - -
4	W. P. Hocken.	4 "		268 - -
5	Nehemiah Stephens	2 "		134 - -
6	A. Hosken.	2 "		134 - -
7	John Bawden.	2 "		134 - -
8	William Phillips	2 "		134 - -
9	Wm Hocken.	2 "		134 - -
10	W. T. Honman.	2 "		134 - -
11	Richd. Hocken	2 "		134 - -
12	Wm Robling	2 "		134 - -
13	Richd Townsend	2 "		134 - -
14	A. S. Lidgey	2 "		134 - -
15	George Truscott.	2 "		134 - -
16	W. M. Cordell.	2 "		134 - -
17	John Martin	2 "		134 - -
18	Thos Pearce	2 "		134 - -
19	Chas Sweet	2 "		134 - -
20	Thos Courtis	2 "		134 - -
21	Nath. Hocken	2 "		134 - -
22	Miss Salmon	1 "		67 - -
23	John Hill	2 "		134 - -
24	John Jenkins	1 "		67 - -
25	J. L. Hocken Senr	1 "		67 - -
26	J. L. Hocken	1 "		67 - -
27	Ed. Hocken	1 "		67 - -
28	John Hocken	1 "		67 - -
29	William Hocken	1 "		67 - -
30	S. R. Serpole.	1 "		67 - -
	Ship Balance in J. H. Hocken debit			65 17 5
				£ 4353 17 5

24 Initial shareholders in the *Ocean Ranger* of 1875, from her account-book. Built at Appledore in that year, she voyaged to the Cape of Good Hope and across the Indian Ocean to Adelaide. At 281 tons, she was the Hocken family's second largest barquentine, earning her cost in her first ten years and sold in 1904.

similar sloop, the *Penquite*, built that year by Marks & Rendle. Rendle, too, built the schooner *Rachael Anne* of 1841 of which Edward was master and principal owner.

A few years later they bought their first square-riggers, Prince Edward Island built — the three-year old *Fortune Teller* by Nathaniel from a Newport shipbuilder; and by Nathaniel and John Henry the brand new 130-ton brigantine *Catherine*. Through the 1850s and 1860s there followed, among others, the brigantines *Concord* (1858), *Wild Wave* (1861), both PEI-built, the *Jane & Ann* (1865) and the *Dashing Wave* (1868).

Variously described as master mariner, ship chandler and bank agent, John Henry (d. 1892) was usually recorded as managing owner of the family ships, along with his elder brother Nathaniel (d. 1900), his son the sailmaker John Edward (d. 1912) and John Henry's son-in-law, another Polruan master mariner, William Francis Hannan. By founding in the 1880s the Fowey shipbrokers Hannan, Samuel & Company, Hannan ensured the continuity of the family tradition in the port for at least another hundred years.

'PLANTATION-BUILT' SHIPS

Various leading local families other than the Hockens put their money on the big softwood vessels then being built in Canada where there were limitless supplies of cheap timber. In all 44 were acquired at one time or another, mainly direct but some via owners in other home ports, all but seven of them between 1841 and 1880 (Appendix 'G'). They originated in Prince Edward

26 The barquentine *Ada Peard* built for Nathaniel Hocken at Par by Samuel Moss 1875, 256 tons. She was to and fro across the Western Ocean for forty years. Only just bought by the Slade family, she was wrecked on the coast of Nova Scotia 1916. A painting by de Simone of Naples.

Island, Nova Scotia, New Brunswick and Quebec, the principal source being the first-named, contributing 34 of them, some built by shipwrights who had emigrated from Bideford and Northam in Devon, as told in *West countrymen in Prince Edward's Isle* by Greenhill & Giffard.

American oak had begun to be imported into England from Canada in 1763 but for shipbuilding had been found to be subject to early decay, a fault shared by wood from the Baltic. The Canadian ships were

25 Remedy for the cholera, an *aide memoire* jotted in the account book of schooner *Rachael Anne* of 1841.

constructed mainly from the species of larch most widely distributed in North America, called variously tamarack, hackmatack and (by *les Canadiens*) *épinette rouge*, strong and readily steamed and bent to shape. A certain number of these craft were built by William Richards for James Yeo of Port Hill, New Bideford, PEI, to a design that, to ease the storage of cargo, dispensed with beams in the hold, having beams only in the cabin and in the way of each mast. In the Fowey yards a number of them were strengthened and refastened with copper bolts and sheeting.

One of the largest of these archaically called 'Plantation-built' ships acquired by Fowey/St. Austell/Liskeard merchants was the 553-ton barque *George Arkle* built at Napan, Nova Scotia, in 1861 and bought by William Warren Dingle, but on average they were about 150 tons. As the years of build and demise of 26 of them can be found on the Fowey register, it is possible to get some idea of their longevity, which averaged 20½ years compared with the average life of all ships on the register at the end of 1850, 39 years. They were employed mainly on deep water and especially to Newfoundland.

Fowey's biggest sailing vessels rarely seem to have brought their owners much luck. The largest ever was the 761-ton barque *Bangalore*, Jersey-built in 1843 and owned by the merchants Dingle, Drew and Hicks on being transferred to Fowey in 1857. She had to be abandoned at sea that very year. Another example, the largest of the Canadian-built vessels: the barque *Good Intent*, 593 tons, built at Richibucto, New Brunswick in 1842 and bought the following year by Hicks, Drew and Morcom who put her to carrying emigrants. She too had to be abandoned in 1856 off the coast of Newfoundland.

SHIP LOSSES

It is not unlikely that the increasing engagement in the hazards of foreign trade after the Napoleonic wars was the cause of the growth in the proportion of ship losses as the century matured. Of the ships registered between 1786 and 1815 something of the order of 24% were lost at sea (though not all during that period) — foundered, stranded, wrecked, absent, abandoned, went missing, *etc.* — from whatever cause other than seizure or capture. Of those registered between 1816 and 1840 about 43% were similarly lost, and the

proportion rose to as high as 57% of those going on the register in the years 1841—1880.

It appears that, generally speaking, the smaller vessels had a longer expectation of life than the larger — the sloops, yawls, ketches and smacks, the barges and lighters. Many of the smaller vessels had long lives, for example the 50-ton sloop *Standard*, employed mainly to and fro on the Bristol Channel from north Cornwall and Devon to the south Wales coast, built at Fowey 1837, altered to ketch in 1889, dismantled and hulked 1917 — 80 years' service.

During the years to 1840 when Charlestown, Pentewan and Par were built, when harbour improvements were made, and the great Plymouth breakwater took some thirty years to build, the barges and lighters were busy all along the south-east Cornish coast. Some 42 vessels so-called had gone on (and off) the register at Fowey by that time. Though the number fell to nil, it is likely that some of the craft rigged and described as sloops, yawls, ketches and smacks were flat-bottomed, shallow-water craft of the kind. Some were sea-going coastwise, others were more or less confined to river, harbour and canal.

BARGES AND BARGEES

Often owned by local farmers and husbandmen, barges, lighters and small ketches were much employed beteen Fowey harbour and Lostwithiel, where the river was the nearest navigable water to Bodmin, tidal over its seven miles. On spring tides and with difficulty, broad, shallow-draught craft with up to 15 tons could get up to Lostwithiel, where the quays after about 1400 had ceased to be approachable by sea-going ships because of silting up by mining refuse. Throughout the 19th century, timber, often brought into the harbour by Baltic traders, was rafted up-river to wherever it was required.

In the local maritime hierarchy the river-going bargees and lightermen were among the lowliest, and if their labour involved them in less danger than their deep-sea contemporaries, they barely scratched an impoverished living, ekeing out their small earnings by tending vegetable patches, poaching and odd-jobbing. Many lived with their families in a flat, one-time swamp called Goosey Town close by Lostwithiel and the river, described by a writer in the *West Briton* in 1871.

He pictured the houses as dirty, comfortless and dank,

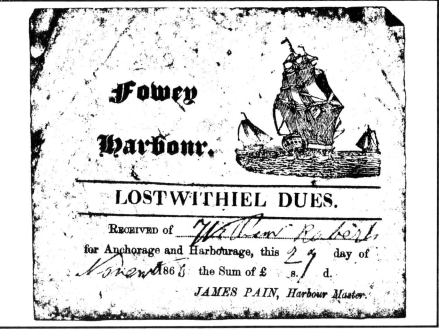

in danger of collapse from gross neglect. The doors and windows creaked and shook 'as though from the cholic or ague'. No paint had passed over them since their carcasses had first been erected. A green fungus hung about the bedroom windows, hardly ever opened, and sometimes an unseemly mixture of the sexes huddled together in the same sleeping room and even in the same bed. The drains were all open, so badly constructed that animal and vegetable matter stagnated in them. 'Though an unfailing supply of fresh water is at hand', the writer said as though with a shudder, 'the rubbish is left to putrefy in the sun. Fish are cleaned within doors, the reeking refuse thrown on dunghill or into cesspool hard by'.

Altogether the description of Goosey Town reminds one of Gustave Doré's grotesque drawings of the London slums at the same date, yet probably little worse than many a poor sailorman of the time endured ashore.

COMING OF THE STEAMERS

It was coincidental that in the middle decades of the 19th century, when many people got the idea that the short cut to making a fortune was to buy shares in ships, and when local investment therein probably reached its peak, two traditional outgoing cargoes carried by the port's ships — pilchards and mineral ores — suffered relapses.

In the pilchard export trade to the Mediterranean steamers were a new element. Though always subject to wild fluctuations in price and catch, the trade nevertheless annually engaged Cornish-owned sailing vessels in large numbers. Pilchards were the main catch of the Cornish fisheries and for them the home market had always been limited. The bulk was sent salted in hogsheads to the Mediterranean ports, especially Italian, with fruit, olive oil and general cargo on the return run. For example in 1847 40,883 hogsheads or 122,000,000 fish were exported.

The first steamship to put into Fowey harbour is said to have been the 170-ton *Sir Francis Drake* of Plymouth in 1825. But it was another thirty years before the first belonged to the port — the 53-ton paddler *Forager*, schooner-rigged, built at Trentport, Nottingham in 1826, and uneasily owned by as many as 23 local people. Her engine room tonnage, by the way, was 66% of the gross which possibly indicates that she was used as a tug. Then in 1858 came the *Albatross*, an iron screw steamer of 109 tons. She was owned by William West

41

who, in a foundry beside the canal at St. Blazey near Par, produced machinery for many mines at home and overseas before closing down in 1891. But, whatever their cargoes, neither vessel lasted long at Fowey. The *Albatross* was sold to Cape Town in 1860 and the *Forager* to Bristol two years later.

By that time the compound engined screw steamers were beginning to cut into the pilchard trade to the Mediterranean, sometimes even via London and Liverpool, thence again by steamer. By 1870 only two cargoes of pilchards caught in the July—December season of that year were carried in sailing vessels. The exceptions went in two fast sailing schooners belonging to William Luke of Charlestown — the 98-ton *Maria Louise*, with 662½ hogsheads, leaving Newquay December 29 and arriving Naples January 12 1881; and the *Racer* with 442 hogsheads, leaving St. Ives on the evening of January 4, arriving Genoa January 18, less than 14 days, at that time believed to be the fastest passage for a vessel of her size, 61 tons.

In the following season, 1871, one of the most productive ever known, the catch was three times the average, and tens of thousands of hogsheads went to the Mediterranean. A salt famine ensued, during which at least one vessel bound under sail for Cornwall with a cargo of salt from Liverpool was speeded on its way by a tow from a steamer. Speed and dependability of delivery were possible by steam to a degree denied to sail, so the pilchard carrying trade went over to the 'steamboats'.

MINING DECLINE AND THE EMIGRANT TRADE

Cornish copper production reached its peak in 1856, and thereafter declined because of competition mainly from Chile and the United States, where output exceeded Cornwall's despite the Civil War. In 1865 of the 325 mines at work in England's two western-most counties only six were paying dividends regularly from copper, five from tin and four from lead. The financial crisis of 1866 made things worse, and by 1874 mining in the Duchy was in ruins.

The impact of all this on shipments out of Fowey was probably not so bad as from those ports that were more westerly. The mines between St. Austell and the River Tamar were newer and the last to be overcome by the impact of competition. In fact, at Looe it was decided in June 1861 to increase quay-room to cope with the increasing traffic — more than £4,000 worth of copper ore was lying on the quays there and at times there were as many as 30 vessels in the harbour.

Cornishmen had been emigrating especially to the United States and Canada from the time of the Napoleonic wars, intending settlers coming largely from the north and east of the county. The Californian and Australian gold discoveries of 1848 and 1851 then drew scores of miners to the emigrant ships. By the 1860s the decline in mining employment caused many hundreds of families to leave, not merely 'to make their fortunes' but with no thought of ever wanting or being able to return. Many left in small vessels from near their homes, travelling to Bristol and Liverpool where they trans-shipped into larger ones.

Some did sail direct for New York or Quebec from Fowey, Falmouth, Padstow and Penzance. The 410-ton barque *Royal Adelaide*, formerly of Falmouth but of Fowey from 1842 to 1869, was engaged in this trade, under the joint ownership of John Mein, a Fowey gentleman, and John Hicks, the principal merchant of his day on the Polruan side of the harbour. She was one of the Canadian softwood vessels already described, built in Quebec in 1831, 108 feet in length.

On June 12 1850 the *Royal Cornwall Gazette* carried an advertisement to the effect that the well-known, fast-sailing, copper-bolted barque *Royal Adelaide* would

THE BARQUE "GOOD INTENT," OF FOWEY, WARBURTON, MASTER,

MAY be expected to sail again from *Fowey* on her fall voyage about the middle of August. Persons desirous of EMIGRATING will do well to make an early application to Mr. HENRY COUCHE Licensed Emigration Agent, or to Mr. WILLIAM HICKS, Merchant, of Fowey; Mr. JOSEPH DREW, or Mr. JOSEPH MORCOM, St. Austell; Mr. HENRY DREW, Stationer, of Bodmin; Mr. SAMUEL ALLEN, of Mevagissey; Mr. H. TRESTRAIL, of Looe; or to Mr. CHANNON, Innkeeper, Liskeard, from whom full particulars may be known.

The charge for passage, including the legal allowance of provisions, will be as low as any other ship.

Dated June 12, 1850.

28 Advertisement from the *West Briton*, June 14 1850, announcing intending departure from Fowey of emigrant barque *Good Intent*, John Warburton master.

29 Emigrant ships leaving the Cattewater, Plymouth — painting by John Callow (1822—1878).

Plymouth City Museum & Art Gallery

leave Fowey for Quebec on about August 3, wind and weather being favourable. She was described as fitted up for passengers in the most convenient and comfortable manner. Would-be emigrants were invited to apply to the captain on board, or to Mr. Bate, Postmaster and Licensed Emigration Agent at Fowey, or to Mr. John Hicks himself. Each passenger would be supplied with provisions as enumerated in the Passenger Act.

When she sailed, in fact on August 12, commanded by Richard Smith, she carried 93 passengers. (Under the 1847 Passenger Act more than 100 would require her to carry a surgeon or to allow each emigrant twelve instead of ten square feet of space). Among them was a Polruan shoemaker and his family. A diary of the voyage was kept by his son, Richard Dingle, whose only criticism, a not unusual one, was of the bread and biscuit served out. 'It is nothing better than Highway Robbery', wrote the young man, 'and I sincerely hope the ship will never again be allowed to put to sea with such bread to be served out to passengers who have paid for such as is used on Her Majesty's ships.....Many of the biscuits are so eaten with the Black Worms they resemble honeycomb, others like flint — water won't penetrate in 24 hours. Conduct in this respect is inconsistent with the principles of honesty...'

As well as Captain Richard Smith (from 1844), masters of the *Royal Adelaide* included Thomas Lenty (from 1842), John Richards (from 1851) and William Facey (from 1855). Between 1855 and 1857 another Fowey merchant, William Warren Dingle, bought control of the vessel, and then in 1869 sold her to John Tredwen of Padstow. Tredwen died in 1870, and two years later the vessel also ended her days, wrecked at Santiago de Cuba. (By the way, she should not be confused with a one-time Falmouth schooner of the same name and period that finished her days as a coal hulk at Fowey, with her transom minus eight letters, so that she became known as the *Adela*).

FOWEY HARBOUR ENTERS CHINA CLAY TRADE

While Cornwall was increasingly pre-occupied with emigration, and the mines were up against odds that were to prove too great for them, mid-century commerce in the eastern part of the county was saved from collapse by the china clay industry. It took a big stride forward in the 1850s, and by 1872 there were over a hundred clay works centred largely on the area around St. Austell and busy as never before. Their output had outgrown the facilities of the havens in St. Austell Bay from which it was shipped — Charlestown, Par and Pentewan. Also by the 1860s the railways were extending to unify the whole district, making points of

shipment available to production sources to an extent denied to horse-drawn wagons, unable to haul over steep gradients. This combination of influences put Fowey's deep-water harbour — the port's biggest single asset and hitherto under-utilised — into the china clay trade.

A Board of Commissioners was set up under an Act of Parliament in 1869 to regulate and develop the harbour. At the same time a minerals railway from Lostwithiel to the harbour was at last opened, with jetties for the loading of ships as there was a lack of suitable quays. Against bitter opposition it had been projected on the promise of iron ore traffic from the Restormel Royal Iron Mine at Lostwithiel. The promise was never fulfilled, barges continued to be used to carry the shrinking output down for trans-shipment to larger vessels at Fowey. Instead the line brought with it the inception of what has been the harbour's main function ever since — the shipment of china clay, especially in vessels of greater draught than could be accommodated in the shallow sub-ports of St. Austell Bay.

In May 1869 the 130-ton schooner *Rippling Wave*, Captain Thomas Roberts, took out the first clay cargo shipped in the harbour (though not, of course, the first shipped from the *port*). It was her maiden voyage. She

30 The *Rippling Wave*, Captain Thomas Roberts, launched from Butson's yard March 27 1869, the first vessel to take out china clay loaded in Fowey harbour. Built for Thomas Halls Knight, a Lostwithiel merchant, she was wrecked in 1907 at South Rock, Co. Down, Ireland. A painting by de Simone *Figlio*, of Naples 1875.

31 A century ago — tiers of sailing vessels lay off the jetties at Fowey harbour awaiting their turn to be loaded with china clay. This, in cask, was horse-drawn by railway truck-load to each jetty head. Of up to 300 tons, such vessels as these took the cargoes to home ports, trans-ocean lots being shipped to others for transfer to larger ships as part-cargo. Subsequently, with the growth of exports, bigger vessels and mechanised loading were introduced.

had been launched on March 27 from the Bodinnick Yard of Nicholas and Joseph Butson, when the christening ceremony was performed by Miss M. Knight of the family of Lostwithiel merchants who were her principal owners. The *Rippling Wave* was loaded prior to the official commencement of service on the Lostwithiel—Fowey railway on June 1 (after which the first to be loaded at the new Carne Point Jetty was the Cardiff brig *Urania*, bound for Cette with 320 tons of clay); but the first engine, pulling three wagons, had travelled on the line on January 11.

The *Rippling Wave* carried her cargo to Genoa and went on to Leghorn and loaded marble for Bristol, arriving there September 5. Edward Rillston became her managing owner June 28 1887, succeeded by Inkerman Tregaskes of Par on February 23 1897. She was in service for thirty-eight years before being wrecked at South Rock, Co. Down, Ireland on March 1 1907.

Captain Thomas Roberts, master of the *Rippling Wave*, who was swept overboard in the Bay of Biscay and drowned on October 10 1878, aged 43, was one of a seafaring family characteristic of the port in those days. Five of his six sons became master mariners. The oldest, Thomas John, succeeded his father at the age of 22 as master of the ship, then went on to command big square riggers belonging to other ports, including the big new Glasgow barque *Dunfion* which in September 1895 took the first china clay cargo direct from Fowey to Philadelphia. In 1907, commanding the full-rigged *Cambuskenneth*, he rescued the crew of an American ship in the Pacific, and in recognition was presented with inscribed binoculars and gold watch by President Theodore Roosevelt. He commanded the ss *Strathness*

32 Request (1895) to Captain William Roberts, Fowey, for news of the schooner *Betsy Nicol*. By the time of its receipt she and her sister ship, *Louisa*, as well as the addressee, had been lost off Land's End.

William & Louise Langlois, San Francisco

till 1914, then HMT *Polgarth* till 1919 when he retired, dying in April 1948. Altogether he rounded Cape Horn twenty-two times. His son William Reginald was also a master mariner.

Of this Polruan family there was another branch of whom William Roberts was co-owner and master of the Fowey schooners *Louisa* and *Betsy Nicol*. He and his

33 Mevagissey's inner harbour in the 1920s with the schooner *Snow Flake* of Runcorn tied up at the quay. A Northcountryman, with a typical local hull-form, she was built at Runcorn in 1880, was to and from Newfoundland for many years, then in the home trade mainly with china clay and coal.

son were drowned when both vessels were lost 'side by side' off Land's End on voyage from Cork to Swansea in December 1894.

By 1876 Fowey harbour was shipping half as much china clay and stone again as Par and more than three times as much as Charlestown. 'Great activity prevails in the shipment of china clay', reported the *West Briton* from Fowey in November 1874, 'and not the slightest delay takes place in the loading of the vessels'. These were under sail, of course, steamers were still unusual, bringing coal from South Wales or taking iron ore for Middlesbrough.

Over the years trading into and out of the port involved an increasing number of vessels belonging elsewhere. The ledger of one china clay company shipping from Par and Charlestown bears witness that by the 1870s almost as much of it was carried in non-Cornish vessels as in Cornish-owned ones. Their home ports were mostly on the west coast — Maryport, Barrow, Fleetwood, Runcorn, Cardigan. In the first half of the century the commonest trading pattern at Fowey appears to have been to South Wales with mineral ore (copper, tin, lead, iron) and coal and culm (for the limekilns) on the return. In the second half it was replaced by china clay and stone to the Potteries via the Mersey, and coal on the return from Scotland as well as Wales.

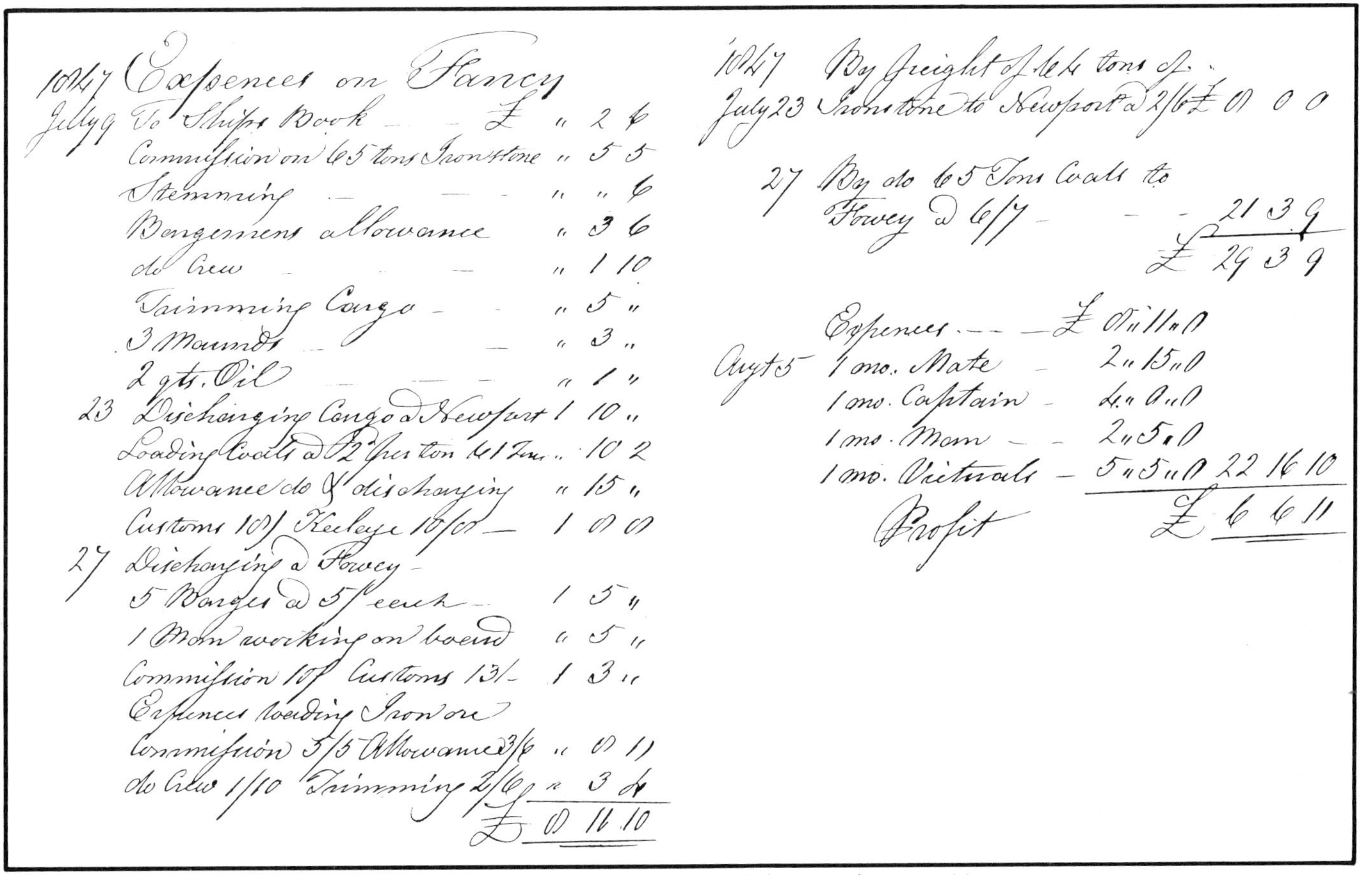

1847 Expences on Fancy
July 9 To Ships Book — £ " 2 6
    Commission on 65 tons Ironstone " 5 5
    Stemming " " 6
    Bargemens allowance " 3 6
    do Crew " 1 10
    Trimming Cargo — " 5 "
    3 Maunds " 3 "
    2 qts. Oil — " 1 "
  23 Discharging Cargo d Newport 1 10 "
    Loading Coals d 2/ per ton 61 Tons 10 2
    Allowance do & discharging " 15 "
    Customs 10/ Keelage 10/6 1 0 0
  27 Discharging d Fowey
    5 Barges d 5/ each 1 5 "
    1 Man working on board " 5 "
    Commission 10/ Customs 13/- 1 3 "
    Expences loading Iron ore
    Commission 5/5 Allowance 3/6 " 0 11
    do Crew 1/10 Trimming 2/6 " 3 4
    £ 8 16 10

1847 By freight of 64 tons of
July 23 Ironstone to Newport d 2/6 £ 8 0 0
  27 By do 65 Tons Coals to
    Fowey d 6/7 — 21 3 9
    £ 29 3 9

    Expences — £ 8 11 0
Augt 5 1 mo. Mate — 2 15 0
    1 mo. Captain — 4 0 0
    1 mo. Man — 2 5 0
    1 mo. Victuals — 5 5 0 22 16 10
    Profit £ 6 6 11

34 Accounts of sloop *Fancy* July 9—August 5 1847. Her length was 48 feet and she carried a crew of four.

SOME MID-CENTURY CARGOES

A few account and cargo books for a number of little Fowey vessels characteristic of the mid-century period have survived, and perhaps reflect the changing pattern of trade. Between 1845 and 1851 the principal cargoes of the 50-ton smack *Mary Ann & Eliza* were coal (2,517 tons), culm (934), copper and iron ore (2,443), limestone (383), china clay and stone (133). Between 1847 and 1855 the main cargoes of the 62-ton sloop *Fancy* were coal (3,435 tons), culm (832), mineral ore (2,159), ironstone (1,092) and limestone (640). Both vessels traded only to points between Plymouth and Llanelly.

We also have rather later figures for three coasting schooners, calling at Continental as well as home ports. From 1852—1857 the 97-ton *Trewartha* mainly carried coal (2,000 tons), china clay in cask and bulk (1,964), salt (1,019), pig iron (450), iron ore (431). Between 1861 and 1865 the principal cargoes of the 57-ton *Rachael Anne* were china clay (1,095 tons), coal (1,081), salt (441), ore (357) and pig iron (350).

Still later, from 1877—1887, the main cargoes of the 111-ton *Maggie C* were coal (7,047 tons), china clay and stone (6,362), mineral ores (1,254) and salt (1,224).

The figures for these vessels reflect the dependability of coal as a cargo, the contraction of mineral ore and the expansion of china clay. Of course each took other subordinate cargoes. The *Maggie C*, for example, took stone, soda, bricks, cement, bones, cereals, phosphate, railway rails and chairs, fish plates, pipes, iron, coal-tar pitch, seedcake and sandalwood. Her account book, for the duration of her existence, ten years, is in the

35 Ports of call at which disbursements were made by sloop *Fancy* July 14 1862 to April 6 1863.

Fowey Town Museum. A transcript of it, detailing cargoes, voyages and earnings is at Appendix 'J'.

SHIPS' AND CREWS' EARNINGS

The accounts of these vessels suggest little better than subsistence earnings. It is true that, as the appendix in *The Merchant Schooners* shows, in her lifetime, May 1873 — March 1877, the 175-ton schooner *Thetis* of Fowey earned a return of nearly 13%, but her profitability towards the close of the period was less than half of what it was at the beginning, probably because of the fall in freight rates after 1873 when they had climbed to a peak.

The *Thetis* in 1873 cost £3,705 or about £21 per gross ton. The *Maggie C*, built at Dysart by Watt in November 1876, salted and classed A1, cost £2,000 or about £18 per gross ton. By her time, the china clay trade was suffering a setback. More important, the whole country was already immersed in what came to be called 'The Great Depression', lasting until 1893, when the word *unemployment* first found its way into the dictionary and when prices and rents fell so much that by 1886 the £ was able to buy more than at any time since 1793 — or later.

On July 2 1887 the *Maggie C* was run into in the Bristol Channel by the ss *Dordogne* of Cardiff and sank near Nash Point. Captain Nathaniel Crews Stevens Couch, her master and owner of 55 of her 64ths, valued her in this her tenth year at £1,261. His claim was settled for £975 which, with balance from voyages, came to £982. After law and other costs were deducted, the amount to share among the owners was £865 or £13.50 per 64th 'in full settlement of all claims and liabilities whatsoever'. This final distribution, plus the earnings over the whole period of £18.32 per share, totalled £31.82 per share. This meant that the owners, after ten years and carrying some 25,000 tons of cargo, in all received only £0.57 more per share than had originally been paid for the ship.

In the four years 1845 — 1848 the *Mary Ann & Eliza* made 32 voyages that earned £137. Between July 1847 and January 1849 the *Fancy* earned a total of £4. The *Rachael Anne* from May 1861 to April 1864 made £50. And these were years when conditions were favourable.

Wages and victuals for the crews of these three 50/60-ton vessels were a good deal less than the £26 a month that they totalled for the 111-ton *Maggie C*, running out at between £14 and £17 a month. The master of each of the smaller vessels was paid £4 a month, the mate about £2.75 and the seamen £2.

Usually the managing owner received a gratuity or percentage for his services — anything from £1 to £3 per annum. And the master could usually make 'a bit on the side' from personal cargo.

Like farming, these little vessels were a way of life that afforded its followers a status or other advantages that they otherwise might not have had. Alternative employment — on fishing craft or farm, in mine or clay pit — was often not available to youngsters, and when it was it was not always preferred. Becoming apprenticed to a craftsman such as shipwright or blacksmith was largely a matter of who one's father was.

The money figures of those days may seem paltry, but the wages and victuals that totalled about £1.60 per man per week in the *Maggie C* were little different from a working landsman's weekly pay (though more than half the country's manual workers received below that sum). A pint of porter could be had for a penny or so, and a small but well-built house could be bought freehold for less than £100. Here and there a seaside cottage still stands that was built by a frugal shipmaster out of the savings from his voyages, perhaps still even bearing the name of the vessel that earned him the money.

36 Its foundation stone laid in 1830, Par harbour was built by Joseph Thomas Austen (later Treffry) to ship the products of the mines, clay pits and granite works. It soon took precedence over Charlestown and Pentewan. Here are vessels berthed there with the tug *Treffry* pre-1914, iron-built in 1870, twin-engined, single screwed, and for over sixty years owned by the family after whom she was named.

COMING OF TUGS

When the rich were richer and the poor were poorer, the expansion of trade generated by the competition that followed the ending of monopolies like the East India Company, the opening of British ports to foreigners, and the scrapping of scores of import and Excise duties, both demanded and resulted from the railways and other transportation improvements of many kinds, most of them long since taken for granted.

For example, for over fifty years after Waterloo there was no tug in the whole port of Fowey. Contrary winds kept vessels idle in and out of harbour, and in a calm they could be moved only by warping or by hiring hobblers (sometimes 'hovellers') to tow them either by rowing or by hauling from land.

The port's first steam tug went into service in 1870, a few months after the outbreak of the Franco-Prussian war — the iron-built, screw-propelled *Treffry*, 46 tons, 63 feet, launched at Paisley earlier that year. She was clinker built and smack rigged. The combined power of her twin engines was 25 hp. Among her first owners was Edward John Treffry (d. 1880) of Place, Fowey, Clerk in Holy Orders, Doctor of Civil Law, who between 1854 and 1876 had shares for varying periods in about forty Fowey vessels.

The *Treffry* worked out of Par harbour for many years, at first for a variety of owners belonging to that place, or to Charlestown and St. Austell. Charles Remfry, a Par

37 A schooner, possibly the *Dashwood*, takes a tow from the tug *Treffry* through the mouth of Par harbour, 1897.

accountant, was her managing owner till he died in 1886 and another, Inkerman Tregaskes, succeeded him. Among the principal shareholders were the merchants, Treffry and Clunes. Charles Ebenezer Treffry gradually bought out all the others by 1912. Until 1920, for thirty-five years, her master was Captain Samuel William Tregaskes. She was sold to a Portsmouth shipbreaker and, soon after, in 1934, was lost by stranding off Dunkirk.

Where tugs today only occasionally go beyond port limits, in the days of sail they steamed many miles to

give tow to vessels becalmed, to ferry pilots, and sometimes to save lives. On occasion a visiting ship might oblige another with a tow but this practice was frowned upon as it resulted too often in accidents. The *Treffry* normally worked up-Channel to the Start and down-Channel as far as the Lizard, collecting small vessels and sometimes towing up to four at a time. Her main job was to tow in and out of Par, Charlestown and Pentewan harbours, less frequently out of Looe, Polperro and Mevagissey.

Fowey harbour, which took ocean-going craft of greater draught than could the others, had no steam tug of its own till the 40-ton *Countess of Jersey* in 1881. She had been launched in Swansea the previous year, clinker built of iron and smack-rigged like the *Treffry*, with two engines giving 34 hp combined. Her owner was a Fowey shipbroker already mentioned, George Bate, and after he died in 1891 he was succeeded by Henry Paull and his Fowey Tug & Salvage Company. She came to her end in the same year as the *Treffry*, 1934, broken up at Penzance.

However, only three years after the arrival of the *Countess of Jersey* in 1884, a second and larger tug the *Gallant*, was acquired and managed by Bate who jobbed off small lots of 64ths to each of thirteen other people. She too was clinker built of iron, by the Rother Iron Works of Rye, Sussex. Her twin engines generated 80 hp. In 1903 her tonnage was increased from 69 to 76 and her length from 77 feet to 86 feet.

The *Gallant* served Fowey for all of seventy years under changing ownership involving many local people (23 in 1903), notably the same Fowey Tug & Salvage Company. Ultimately, she was sold by the Harbour Commissioners in 1954 to a Torpoint lighterage concern.

Appropriately bearing the ancient nick-name of citizens of Fowey, the *Gallant* was known all along the south Cornish and Devon coasts, where her dependability and trim condition inspired an unusual degree of public affection.

MEMORABLE DEEP-SEA VESSELS

The period 1840 to 1880 saw the launch of many other vessels that lasted into the memories of people still living, vessels commemorated on cottage walls by modest representations done in oil or watercolour for great-grandfather, products of the brush of such ship painters as de Simone of Naples, Louis Renault of Leghorn, Edouard Adam of l'Havre, or more probably our own prolific Reuben Chappell of Par. Often of less than 100 tons, many of these merchantmen traded regularly two thousand miles or more from home, usually with a crew you could count on one hand, ultimately to leave their timbers in distant waters.

There were the schooners: the 82-ton *Brenton*, built at Mevagissey in 1861 and lost at Smoky Tickle, Labrador in 1900; Simon Truscott's *Julia*, 89 tons, built in 1870, lost off Costa Rica 1907, the same year that the South

38 Three barquentines, probably Hocken's, at anchor in Fowey harbour c. 1885, with the tug *Countess of Jersey* in attendance. The tide is very low, and they may be awaiting higher water before berthing without fear of going aground. The Hocken family were managing owners of six ocean-going barquentines: *E.S. Hocken, Ocean Ranger, Ocean Spray, Ada Peard, Ocean Traveller* and *Dashing Wave*, as well as other vessels.

Mr. J.H. Samuel

39 The tug *Gallant*, iron-built at Rye in 1884, in service at Fowey for seventy years until sold in 1954. Lengthened in 1903, she was managed successively by George Henry Bate, Henry Arthur Paull, John Louis Toyne, and then taken over by Fowey Harbour Commissioners in 1951.

40 Contemporary model of the *Brenton*. Built by Nicholas Lelean at Mevagissey in 1861, 83 tons, she was in the Newfoundland trade for many years. Owned mainly by Richard Harris Williams, a St. Austell mining engineer, she passed to John Stephens in 1893 and was lost on the Labrador coast 1900.

Mevagissey & District Museum Society

American trader *Touch-me-not* of 1841 finished up nearer home, as a coal hulk at Dartmouth; the little *Isabella* of 1865, only 61 tons, 'pet and baby' of the Stephens fleet, the most consistent passage-maker in the Newfoundland trade, wrecked in 1913 at the entrance to St. John's. John Henry Hocken's *Sparkling Wave*, Polruan built in 1866, foundering north of the West Indies in 1882.

And the barquentines that included the three Polruaners: Hocken's *Ada Peard*, still trading to Newfoundland in 1916 after forty-one years; the *Koh-i-Noor*, 1877, Captain William Smith, lost in 1906 by stranding on a reef at the entrance of Boca St. Nicoleas Aruba, Netherlands West Indies, off the coast of Venezuela; and the *E.S. Hocken* of 1879, still in the Newfoundland trade in 1917.

But many of these copper-bottomed, blue-water craft were short-lived, now unknown, except perhaps to a descendant or two of their master or owner. Two examples: Hocken's barquentine *Ocean Traveller* of 1872, lost on a Caribbean coral reef only six years later, bound from Barbados to Curaçoa; and Captain Peter

Tadd's schooner *Emily Ellen* also of 1872, another Newfoundlander; she foundered on passage to Liverpool likewise after only six years' service.

THE STEPHENS FLEET

It was in these bullish mid-century years that what became the port's perhaps best-known fleet was founded by a shipbroker of Charlestown and Par, John Stephens (1832 — 1902). He began it in 1867 when he bought shares in the brigantine *Jane*, built at Crapaud, Prince Edward Island the previous year, and it ended in 1939 when the family sold the far-famed *Waterwitch* barquentine. It was at its zenith in 1902, with 17 vessels averaging 130 tons apiece.

Stephens was a big man (over 300 lb) who had faith in little ships and so-named many of them — *Little Wonder, Little Mystery, Little Pet* etc. — so that many people thought that if a vessel had *Little* in her name she was one of his. For much of the year all his *Littles* except one traded between Newfoundland and the Mediterranean, carrying dried cod or salt — fast sailing 'fish boxes' — and in winter months in home waters

41 Launched by John Stephens from Polruan 1875, the *Little Beauty*, 90 tons, first of his fleet of *Littles* of which there were ten, all but one in the Newfoundland/Mediterranean trade — dried codfish east to Europe, salt west. Usually commanded by Edward or Thomas Coombes, she traded for fourteen years till missing in January 1889 between Portugal and Mevagissey.

with china clay, coal or potatoes from Scotland. Stephens of Par was one of the last merchant fleets privately owned by a British family.

Though neither craftsman nor seaman, John Stephens knew a good vessel when he saw one, and in 1874 he entered the ranks of the port's shipbuilders. Employing a brilliant head shipwright named William Ferris (1826 — 1911) he laid down the schooner *Flying Spray* on the beach at his native Charlestown. He then moved to Fowey where, from the site occupied today by the yacht club, he launched four more vessels — the *Ocean Swell, Katie Cluett, Spin-away* and *Emeline Jenkin* — plus a fifth, the *Little Beauty*, from the Polruan shore. All but one, the *Emeline Jenkin*, were star performers.

So far as it is possible to judge, it was in the middle forty years of the 19th century that the port's builders did their best work. At Charlestown, Stephens had, in effect, taken over from Anthony (d. 1859) and William Luke (d. 1871) of the family of merchants of that place who, in 1840, had themselves succeeded William Pearse Banks as occupants of the yard there.

MEVAGISSEY, PAR & LOOE SHIPBUILDERS

Meantime on Mevagissey Bay at Portmellon the Dunn family (whose origins and activities I described earlier) had been building continuously from 1800 to 1842 vessels averaging about 100 tons, cutters in the earlier years and schooners latterly. James Dunn was succeeded about 1835 by Walter. They were related to the Allen family, prominent in Mevagissey's maritime affairs through the 18th and 19th centuries, and also with the Leleans, who built in the town for fifty years from about 1823.

The Lelean family's last vessel was probably the schooner *Beatrice* of 1874 launched on the same day as the *Perseverance* by Benjamin Harris Roberts who, with his brother Henry, built schooners and luggers at Portmellon, after the Dunns, between about 1864 and 1874. Joseph Davis Lelean's *Beatrice* was wrecked on the Newfoundland coast in 1880. The *Perseverance*

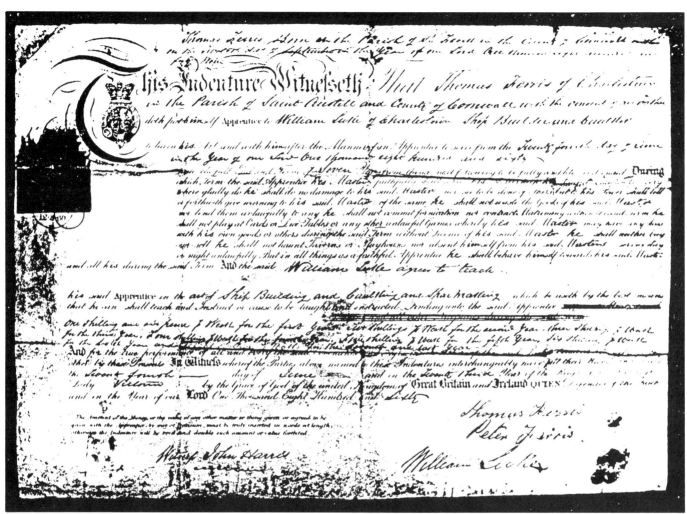

42 Indenture of June 24 1860 binding Thomas Ferris (b 1848) apprentice to William Luke, shipbuilder and caulker of Charlestown, signed by his father Peter Ferris (1826—1911), chief shipwright of, among others, the *Flying Spray, Ocean Swell, Little Beauty, Katie Cluett,* *Spin-away* and *Emeline Jenkin.* Thomas's brother Peter became a yacht and boat builder at Looe. *Mr. Percy Ferris, Polruan*

traded until 1917 when she was sunk by enemy action in the English Channel.

At Par shipbuilding, as distinct from repair work, seems to have begun no earlier than the 1860s with the launch of the 124-ton schooner *Lizzie Trenberth* from the yard owned by Samuel Moss, a St. Austell merchant who employed Richard Tregaskes as his chief shipwright. Tregaskes built seven more schooners and two barquentines for Moss, who signed the certificates as the master builder. Richard's son, Benjamin Moss Tregaskes, was apprenticed at the yard, served at sea and worked for a spell in America.

Another entrant to shipbuilding in these middle years was Henry Shapcott and Son at East Looe, turning out at least eight vessels in 1841 — 1869 averaging about 96 tons apiece, and no doubt other craft of less than the statutory 15 tons. His largest were the 198-ton, 3-mast 'barquette' *Florence* to which I have already referred, and the schooner *Fanny Buller*, launched in February 1859 from a 400-foot way down the beach — 'A set of Captain Marryat's signal flags was presented by Mr. Pole Carew and a full length figure-head by Mr. Buller'. Henry Shapcott died on October 7 1873, leaving Robert Henry to carry on with repair work and boat building.

Abraham Pengelly was another builder at Looe, on the west bank, but I can trace only one merchant vessel to him, the schooner *St. George* of 1867.

BUILDING ON FOWEY HARBOUR

To round off this mid-century tally I must return to Fowey harbour where, as I have said, the Nickels family built for longer than any other, from some time before 1786 down to 1865, 67 identifiable ships over eighty years.

Thomas Nickels the Elder, shipwright, died in 1829 aged 77; Thomas the Younger, mariner, died in 1838 aged 58; another Thomas, master of the *Blanche Moore*, died in

43 The 124-ton *Lizzie Trenberth*, built by Samuel Moss at Par 1867 and managed mainly by Inkerman Tregaskes till the early 1920s, largely in the china clay trade. She went missing after leaving Holyhead in October 1923.

1862 aged 45, on passage from Calcutta. George Nickels, who took over the shipbuilding from 1821 to 1865, died aged about 85 in 1871. He, too, had a son, Samuel, described as a 38 year old shipbuilder in 1841, but to him I can trace no particular vessel and he probably worked alongside his father.

The other builder on the west side of the harbour was William Brokenshaw, who was at work from 1813 to 1857 when he died on November 30, a month after the launch of his last and (with *Touch-me-not* of 1841) largest vessel, the *Ann Beer*, 156 tons.

On the east bank of the harbour Marks and Rendle seem to have ceased building after their schooner *William West* in 1846. The registers ascribe some vessels to them jointly and some to each individually. William Rendle was 52 years old in 1851 when he had two shipwright apprentice sons.

At about the time that Marks and Rendle built their last ship, Nicholas Butson (1779 — 1844) died. He had built four schooners at Polruan, and the business was carried on by his two sons as co-partners, Nicholas J. Butson (1818 — 1872) and Joseph William Trudgeon Butson (1822 — 1887). They built both at Polruan and in the yard at Bodinnick formerly occupied by John Marks.

As well as the *Rippling Wave* of 1869, already mentioned, the Butsons built the schooner *Thomas Aylan*, 124 tons, sold for breaking up in 1937 after 77 years' service, the 164-ton brigantine *Gem* of 1871, built at Bodinnick for Captain William Smith of Polruan who traded her to the West Indies and South America; the

44 A vessel in frame at Butson's yard, Bodinnick, about 1870.

45 About 1890, at the entrance to Caffa Mill Pill, Fowey, with Butson's yard on the far bank and, at right, Heller's yard.

173-ton schooner *Thetis* of 1873, wrecked only four years later on the coast of Sardinia; and their last and largest, the 174-ton brigantine *Undine* of 1875 for Thomas Halls Knight, a Lostwithiel merchant who invested in at least half-a-dozen Butson vessels.

The *Undine* was another fast moving West Indiaman, in the pineapple trade. On one occasion (the story is still told) bound from Bristol to St. Michaels she dropped her pilot at Padstow, and there he remained windbound. When at last he did get out he encountered the homing *Undine* and took her into Bristol. She had sailed out to St. Michaels and back in nineteen days. But smart sailing fruiters were ousted by steam. Sold to Whitstable in 1894, she was demoted in old age to the coal trade till 1917 when she was run down by a steamer off Flamborough Head.

46 The schooner *Thetis*, built by Butson 1873 for various local owners, including Luke of Charlestown and T.H. Knight of Lostwithiel. Only four years later she was stranded on the coast of Sardinia, a total wreck.

THE SLADES OF POLRUAN

The Slade famiy of Polruan built larger ships than any other local builder. Their business began with Christopher Slade (1810 — 1870) who, at twenty-one, married Jane Symons Salt, daughter of William Salt, mariner, who owned the Russell Inn in what is now West Street and, close by, a shipwright's yard.

Within five years Christopher was living at the inn, his occupation described as 'Victualler'. In 1841 he bought shares in Edward Hocken's schooner *Rachael Anne* built by William Rendle, and when in the next year he acquired others in his father-in-law's schooner *Alert*, built by Butson, he was described as a shipwright. In 1847 when he bought an interest in the *Fancy*, sloop, he was described as a full-blown shipbuilder. By that time Marks and Rendle had gone out of business.

So, after marrying the daughter of Captain Salt, head of a village family of mariners, landowners and shipowners, he had graduated from keeping a pub to owning and building ships. He may have been a shipwright at the time he married, and for sure had connection (if only through his father-in-law) with Marks, Rendle and Butson, who built vessels in which Captain Salt had a major interest.

But I cannot be sure of any ship by Christopher Slade earlier than the brigantine *Peter & James* of 1856, owned by Peter Tadd and lost on passage from Salonica, 1865. This and others were almost certainly built in the yard below West Street. He launched at least half-a-dozen schooners of from 97 to 157 tons for the Tadds and Hockens, and others, before he died on February 28 1870, aged sixty years.

47 One of the best-known schooners in the china clay trade, the 163-ton *Alert*. Built in 1885 by Brundrit of Runcorn, she was transferred to Fowey from Beaumaris in 1899 when Joseph Waters of Truro was her manager. In 1903 she was again transferred, to Falmouth, and, continuing under Waters's ownership, was engineless till 1938. Re-fitted as a yacht with motor, she was broken up in the war.

48 Men of the shipbuilding yard of J. Slade & Sons, Polruan about 1897. The two bearded men at centre of middle row are, left to right, Samuel and John, sons of Christopher and Jane Symons Slade. Their young nephew, Joseph, is at the extreme right. At bottom right is a guest — identified as Benjamin Moss Tregaskes, on a visit from his yard at Par. He was co-owner of Newquay wet dock at Polruan, rented by Slade's.

Christopher's widow, Jane Symons Slade, was a resolute matriarch. After she had borne him thirteen children, at the age of fifty-seven, she herself took charge of the yard, and from that time traded as J. Slade & Sons. Jane went on being described as 'Shipbuilder' until her death in 1885.

At the time Christopher Slade died they had on the stocks a 149-ton two-mast schooner, and when a few months later she was launched she was named the *Jane Slade* after the new head of the family and firm. Mrs.

Slade retained her majority interest in her, and her son Thomas (and *his* son after him) had command of her, a general deep-sea trader. Re-rigged as a three-master in 1905, she remained on the register until 1928 — fifty-eight years.

Another son, William (d. 1898) is credited with being the chief shipwright of the *Jane Slade* but the yard's mainstay was John Slade until he died in 1909. His daughter Agatha was still living till only a few years ago, an impressive old lady in her nineties.

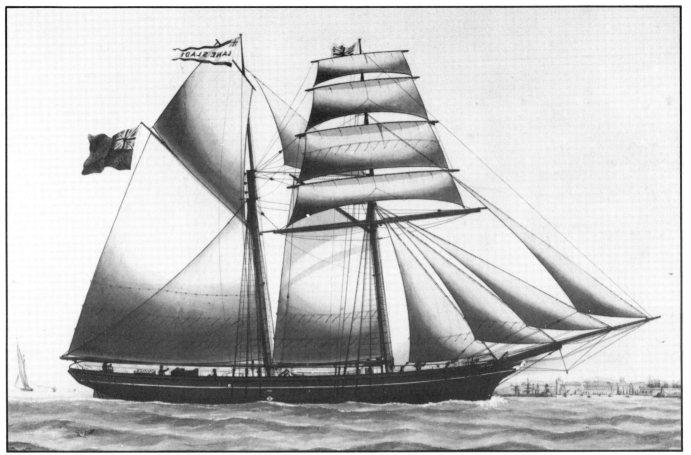

49 Built as a two-mast deep sea trader, the *Jane Slade* as pictured for her master Thomas Slade by Luigi Renault when she was at Leghorn in 1887. Reputed to have made the fastest passage ever from the Azores to Bristol.

H. & B. Graeme, Noah's Ark, Fowey

Yet another son, Samuel, who disabled a hand in a sawpit accident, became the businessman of the family, 'playing the gentleman' as it was put to me by Agatha. He was clerk to the school board throughout its existence, manager and secretary of Polruan's Brazen Island Sardine Company, but lived in more elegant Fowey. There he was a harbour commissioner from 1903 to 1920, dying two years later.

My 11 ships listed as built by Slade's over almost a quarter of a century averaged 168 tons apiece, considerably larger than those of any other builder in the port. The two biggest were both barquentines — the *Koh-i-Noor* of 243 tons, built for Captain William Smith in 1877 (like Butson's *Gem* six years previously);

and in 1879 the *E.S. Hocken*, 296 tons, built for Captain John Henry Hocken. She traded across the Western Ocean for sixty-two years, was over 126 feet long and the last and largest square-rigger built in the whole port, also the last cargo carrier under sail from a Polruan yard.

Twelve months later, in 1880 and from the opposite side of the harbour, the last sailing merchantman of appreciable size to be built in the port was launched and named *Zingari*, 80 tons. This really marked the local end of merchant shipbuilding of wood although, strictly speaking, there was the single exception of a little ketch, *Rival*, built by Richard Heller in 1889. To this there are later references.

60

50 Pilot, fisherman, Methodist and life-saver, Moses Dunn (1839—1920) aboard his yawl *Misfit* (FY184) about 1910 off Polruan. In distance at left is Newquay wet dock with a two-mast schooner *in situ*. The dock was rented by Slade's from its co-owners, Ben Tregaskes of Par and Fortescue's Boconnoc Estate. Behind the schooner's masts is Slade's smithy, rented from about 1924 by a blacksmith, Charles Toms, the beginning of the subsequent boat-building firm of C. Toms & Son, contractors to the Admiralty. The white walled building in the picture was John Edward Hocken's sail loft.

It has sometimes been suggested that *Zingari* laid down on the yacht club site, was built by John Stephens. In fact she was possibly the only merchant vessel built by a Fowey shipowner, Albertus Dingle, in the yard that Stephens had just vacated. He sold her direct to owners in Plymouth, where she was initially registered. From them Stephens bought her in 1888, changing her name to *Little Pet* and transferring her register to her place of origin, Fowey. It could well be that her chief shipwright was the Peter Ferris who had worked for Stephens.

SHIPBUILDING'S END

By 1881, then, in the grip of the Great Depression, the yards of Mevagissey, Charlestown, Par, Fowey, Polruan, Bodinnick and Looe had given up building cargo carriers. Their output had been in decline for many years; economic pressures were demanding larger and larger ships; the 'steamboats' had proved themselves beyond reasonable doubt; and the future was clearly with iron, engineering and coal, natural to the great yards on the Tyne, Wear and Clyde.

There were no material needs of shipbuilding that could be dependably filled from local sources, except perhaps skilled craftsmen, inheritors of a long tradition, and there was ample repairing and boat building work for them, work that called for the kind of financing that was within local means.

On one score alone the yards were unsuited to the construction of the merchant craft of the years to come: their size. They were all small and squeezed, a limitation imposed by the coastal geography. With the possible exception of Par, nowhere between Looe and the Dodman permitted the extent of premises that, in 1860, Richard Tredwen advertised for sale at Padstow on Cornwall's north coast — five acres with a thousand feet of river frontage and three yards capable of building five vessels at a time; a wet and dry repairing dock, two timber ponds, the whole walled with stone and secured by 30-foot gates. Included were workmen's sheds; boat, sail and rigging lofts; a cooper's shop, block shop, a four-forge smith's shop; separate iron, nail, paint and tar cellars; a pitch house, office overlooking the premises; 8-room dwelling house, laundry, stables and coach house, two walled gardens and an acre of 'very best land'

Compared with this, the Fowey builders had managed with little more than the beach.

Nevertheless, long after 1880 there was one short-lived venture. In the 1950s the Channel Islands' Lockett Wilson Line that ran ships to Paris leased Brazen Island, Polruan, and formed Brazen Island Shipyard Ltd. to use its repairing facilities. The availability of first-class craftsmen enabled the firm to build several small steel ships there, including the motor coasters *Vendome* and *Vauban*, also the barge *Mixtow* and the hopper barge *Lantic Bay* for Fowey Harbour Commissioners.

NUMBER OF MERCHANT SHIPS* & TONNAGE BUILT IN THE PORT

	30 years 1786 — 1815	25 years 1816 — 1840	40 years 1841 — 1880
Number of ships* built and registered in the port	301	131	105
.... per annum	15	7	8
Proportion of ships registered that were built in the port	68%	74%	33%
Average tonnage per ship built	75	74	110
Aggregate tonnage built	22,575	9,694	11,550
.... per annum	752	388	289

*including those with no indication of builder's name

The table above is an attempt, by abstraction and analysis of the Fowey Custom House Ship Registers, to summarise shipbuilding in the port during the near-century that ended in 1880. Detail is given in Appendices 'E' and 'F'.

Both the number of ships and the tonnage built declined heavily from the 'Free Trade' days when the yards' mainstay was the need of master smugglers and the Guernsey merchants. By the 1870s output, in both ships and tonnage, was at almost half of what it had once been.

Where over the whole period the tonnage built at Mevagissey suffered the greatest decline, that from the east bank of Fowey harbour enjoyed the greatest increase (Appendix 'E'). The Polruan/Bodinnick output in the 18th century was neglible, but it seems to have exceeded Mevagissey's 1816 — 1840 and to have been bigger in the following forty years than at any other place.

Although prior to 1840 no great difference occurred in the proportion of ships registered that were locally built, in the ensuing forty years it fell radically. Investors found increasingly that they could get a better deal elsewhere than from the yards on their own doorstep, particularly from Devon and eastern Canada.

CHAPTER FOUR
STEAMBOATS, FISHING BOATS, U-BOATS 1881–1920

Of rather more than 1,000 vessels with Cornish connections in the *Merchant Navy List* for 1879 more (129) are shown as having been built in Fowey than in any other port in the Duchy, so that when merchant shipbuilding ceased there effectively in 1880, it amounted to the relinquishment of a leading position. The next most productive were Falmouth and Padstow with 119 apiece.

These 1,000-odd vessels with Cornish connections ranged from 15-ton luggers to 750-ton barques, nearly two-thirds of them schooners averaging about 100 tons. About a quarter had managing owners residing outside the county but the majority were owned where they were registered. The largest number (176) belonged to Fowey. At Falmouth were 128, at Padstow 120, Penzance 78, St. Ives 71, Truro 57, Hayle 30 and Scilly 19.

In the subsequent forty years Fowey's trade expanded along with the Cornish china clay industry, the products of which were its principal cargoes. But the *proportion* of locally-owned vessels engaged in it continued to diminish when measured beside the ever

51 Carrying china clay in cask to Bilbao and San Sebastian, *Deerhound*, 443 tons, built at Millwall 1882, was the second of six steamships, managed by Toyne, Carter & Co. of Fowey and acquired between 1897 and 1902. She was of iron, as were *Norma* (built at Greenock 1877, 507 tons) and *Stockton* (Paisley 1857, 406 tons). The other three were brand new and of steel: *Torfrey* (Paisley 1900, 443 tons), *Par* (Paisley 1902, 436 tons) and *Foy* (Workington 1902, 354 tons). Two were lost in 1902 and 1909, the other four were sold between 1916 and 1927. This fleet was Fowey's chief venture into cargo-carrying steamships.

Mr. Ross Carter, Fowey

growing number registered elsewhere whether under the Red Ensign or foreign flag. Many were so well established in the trade that they were as much part and parcel of it as local ships. For example, at the end of November 1907 the town of Fowey celebrated the hundredth visit for china clay of the Holland Steamship Company's ss *Scheldestroom*. She had a crew of twenty-one and carried 1,600 tons of cargo. Rejoicing changed to mourning only a week later when the tragic news arrived that, on voyage Amsterdam to Plymouth with a cargo of sugar, she had collided with a large sailing ship off Folkestone, was holed and sank.

The average number of ships put on the register at Fowey per annum in this period more than halved (three against eight in much of the previous forty years), indicating decline in local shipping investment.

The near-collapse of local involvement in the ownership of the port's merchant shipping did not occur until after 1900, in the last half of the period with which we are dealing. Although this was certainly induced in part by the cessation of merchant shipbuilding in the area, local people for twenty years after that still put money into vessels, vessels that had been built elsewhere.

As many Scots-built ships as Cornish were bought; and while none came from Plymouth, Fowey's immediate neighbour to the east, her neighbour to the west, Falmouth, was the chief source in Cornwall, equating the yards of Kingsbridge and Salcombe in Devon. These had been built especially for the fruit trade over a long period of years — sharp, fast, spick-and-span vessels that were now largely ousted by steam from the business for which they were designed. Between 1885 and 1912 some ten vessels went on the Fowey register that had been so built, some modified for the Newfoundland trade. They included Rillston's *Spring* and *Shepherdess*; Stephens' *Daring, Pass By, Island Maid, Little Wonder, Little Mystery* and *Little Gem*; also *Titania* and *Sarah*. But with the exception of the three *Little*'s, which were new; all were thirty years or so old.

In this forty year period the Stephens fleet alone added sixteen vessels — and lost fourteen of them, in part by war. That fleet was at its largest in 1902 when its founder, John Stephens, died. Prominent among other local owners and managers at this time were the Couch and Kellow families at Pentewan, and at Fowey George

Henry Bate, Charles Louis Toyne, John Peers Carter and William Francis Hannan, all shipbrokers. Also at Polruan were the Hocken and Tadd families of master mariners; the Johns family of mariners at Mevagissey; Edward Rillston, the Fowey grocer; the Marshalls, mariners, of Looe; Benjamin Moss Tregaskes, the Par shipbuilder and many more.

FOWEY REGISTER 1905—1910

By the beginning of the present century the average tonnage of Fowey's ships had increased to 124 gross, some 37% higher than it had been in 1850. This was due not only to the addition of steamers. By December 31 1905, the port's 101 vessels included 91 under sail, averaging 112 tons, where, half a century earlier, the average had been 78 tons. The 10 steamers averaged 230 tons but included two yachts, *Skirmish* (13 tons) of 1903 and *Sparkle* (68) of 1905, also the three tugs *Treffry* (46) of 1898, *Countess of Jersey* (40) of 1881 and the *Gallant* (76) of 1903.

52 Charles Phillips Couch (1886—1968), Pentewan shipbroker, in the First World War when serving in *HMS Vivid*, Devonport. His grandfather Nathaniel Couch, a master mariner, founded the family business early in the 19th century, and was succeeded by his son Theophilus William Couch. They managed various vessels, notably (of Fowey) the *Mary Miller, Polly & Emily* and *Conoid*.

The inclusion in the official return of *Skirmish* as a steamer is at least of doubtful correctness. Described on her register as an auxiliary screw yawl, she was from birth driven by a petrol engine made by Sim's Manufacturing Co. Ltd. of Bermondsey, London 6BHP. Those were the days when the internal combustion engine in marine craft was in its infantcy, and eight years were to pass before any similar powered vessel went on the register. She was built in 1902 by Henry Roberts of Mevagissey for a St. Austell solicitor and banker, and apparently performed creditably for various owners until in 1957 she was sold to France.

As at December 31 1905, there were five iron or steel-hulled cargo carriers, steam propelled: *Stockton* (407 tons) of 1897, built at the place of that name in County Durham 1857; *Deerhound* (420) of 1898, built at Millwall 1892; *Torfrey* (443) of 1900, built at Paisley in that year; *Par* (436) of 1902, also Paisley-built that year; and *Foy* (354) of 1902, launched that year at Workington. These constituted the port's one and only major venture into steam management, initiated by the shipbrokers Toyne, Carter & Co. in the form of Fowey and Par steamship companies.

This fleet in all was of six ships but the *Norma* (507) of 1899, built at Greenock 1877, had had to be abandoned off Trevose Head on January 28 1902. The Spanish ss *Elantscobe* towed her but she finally sank off Land's End on February 4.

At the end of 1905 the largest vessel under sail was the *E.S. Hocken* (296 tons), and the one that had been longest on the register was the *Richard & Jane*, a 51-foot sloop built by William Brokenshaw in 1829 and first registered in that year. She is the longest-lived Fowey vessel I can find. Her register was closed in 1926 when she was falling to pieces in the ownership of Henry Paull, Fowey tug owner — ninety-seven years' service. Even so there were longer lived craft elsewhere, notably the similar sloop *Ceres* of Bude, launched at Salcombe in 1811 and in service for 125 years.

But by 1910, of the 91 sailing vessels at the end of 1905, as many as a quarter had either gone out of business or had been transferred elsewhere.

Another indicator of local ship-owning decline: over a century, relative to those of neighbouring Plymouth, Fowey's ships positively shrank in the aggregate. Where, at the close of the 18th century, the tonnage of ships of the port of Plymouth was about three times larger than Fowey's, by the beginning of the 20th century it was fourteen times larger.

DEEP-SEA TRADERS

The last years of the 19th century were a period of unprecedented change in the world's shipping lanes. The development of the compound engine and the opening of the Suez Canal in 1869, and its use by steamers, had given them such advantage that the big, full-rigged clippers had been switched to the Australian, New Zealand and South American runs, and even of these they were now beginning to see the end.

Coaling stations — wood to composite, to iron and now to steel construction — twin screws — triple expansion engines — all contributed to a revolution that, working down in its influence to the modest craft of little ports like Fowey, squeezed out many a ship from deep-sea trades and into coasting where, in the days before the ubiquitous motor lorry, there was still money to be earned by water.

Many a vessel like the Fowey-built barquentine *Ocean Swell* that had traded to Brazil for coffee, the Bahamas for 'pines' and the Levant for oil and dates was now pulled out and pushed into such home freights as coals and china clay. Others left their bones a long way from home, and were never replaced, like the 243-ton barquentine *Koh-i-Noor* in 1906 in the Netherlands West Indies. She had been built by Slade's in 1887 for Captain William Smith, principal of the initial owners, twenty all told, whose names included Hicks, Williams, Dingle, Luke, Hocken, Rundle and Morcom. A Polruan widow, Mary Hicks Hayes, became her managing owner in 1880.

Of similar family ownership was the brigantine *Gem*, 164 tons, built by Butson at Bodinnick six years previous to the *Koh-i-Noor*. She, too, traded to the West Indies and South America and, on the death in 1879 of Captain William Smith, also came under the widow's management. In 1895 the vessel was put up for sale by Captain William Charles Smith and was bought by John Edward Hocken, the Polruan sailmaker. Two years later she was sold to owners at Gloucester, to which port she was transferred.

Captain Smith's eighteen months' diary of the *Gem's* voyages and cargoes 1886—1888 is a fair sample of the kind of toil such wide-ranging work-horses did before they were squeezed out and into the home trade:

> October 18 1886: Left Fowey with granite for Malta, thence to Marathonisi, Greece, then with valonia to Fowey for orders. Thence to Bridgwater. Voyage finished March 1887. Towed to Cardiff, loaded coal for Curaçao, thence to Aruba and back to London. To Fowey for half-time survey. Sailed from Fowey September 29 1887 to load patent fuel for La Guayra (Venezuela), thence to Galveston to load oilcake. Sailed from Galveston for Plymouth January 27 1888. Anchored Plymouth Sound March 25 1888.

DEEP SEA PROFITS

Among the most successful deep-sea traders, with draught unsuitable to coasting, were the barquentines of 200—300 tons under the management of Nathaniel,

John Henry and John Edward Hocken. (Appendix 'K'). The contraction of the distributed cash profits of three of them, the accounts of which survive, through the 1880s and 1890s reflects the pressure of competition in this period and, in one case, the subsequent trade revival pre-1914.

In her first five years from 1877 the *Ocean Spray* averaged a profit per annum of £509. In her second five years it was £332. In her third five years (to 1892) it was £166. In her last nine (to 1901) it was £149.

In twenty-four years to 1901, and after paying for the ship's 'first cost' (£5,248), she had made for her owners £1,140. But by November 1903 there were liabilities of £1,213 which were met by acceptance of an offer for

53 Profits summary of the *Ocean Spray*, 1877—1901, from her account-book.

her and a call on shareholders for the balance. The price of £1,010 was low but shareholders were advised: 'Considering the state of shipping and her unsuitable draught for coasting, your committee thought it best to accept this offer than to make a heavy call to put her to sea again'.

The *Ocean Ranger*'s pattern 1876—1900 was much the same: a profit averaging £540 per annum in her first ten years to 1885; of £310 per annum to 1890, and of £166 for each of her last ten years to 1900. She had earned her 'first cost' (£4,353) in her first ten years, but by August 1904, she was in debt by £292 (liabilities of £678 against profits on three voyages of £385). She was sold to a Manchester master mariner for £1,100, and the balance of £807 was paid out to shareholders, £12.12s.3d per 64th.

54 Fowey harbour July 1901. At left is the five-mast schooner *Rebecca Palmer* of Boston, 2,556 tons, 260 feet long. Launched that year, she was on her maiden voyage to Fowey via Le Havre, Rouen and Plymouth, the first five-master to cross the Atlantic and the largest sailer to enter Fowey harbour. Astern of her is the *Ernot Alfred* of Riga.

National Maritime Museum

The *E.S. Hocken*, too, did very well in her first ten years 1880—1889, her distributed profits all but paying for her 'first cost' of £5,248, thus:

5 years to 1884 profit averaged £756 p.a.
5 years to 1889 profit averaged £265 p.a.
5 years to 1894 profit averaged £224 p.a.
5 years to 1899 profit averaged £166 p.a. (re-metalled 1896)
5 years to 1904 profit averaged £121 p.a. (re-metalled 1900).

In six years to 1910, by which time trade was looking up. her owners received an average per annum of £122 despite the cost of re-metalling in both 1905 and 1908 and of re-trenailing in 1910. Then in 1911, their profit jumped to £384. Moreover, she subsequently earned good profits-on-voyage: £820 between October 1911 and September 1912, Glasgow — St. John's — Pernambuco — Barbados — St. John's — Harbour Grace — Glasgow — Exmouth — Fowey.

Built within four years of each other these three barquentines varied a bit in their initial cost per ton. *Ocean Ranger*, built at Appledore 1875, was cheapest at £15.49; *Ocean Spray*, built by Moss at Par in 1877, cost £19.65; and, *E.S. Hocken*, built by Slade at Polruan 1879, was half-way between the two at £17.72.

All three traded to much the same places and points between: the West Indies and down to Montevideo in the South Atlantic, ports of south-eastern USA, Newfoundland and western Europe. But, exceptionally, the *E.S. Hocken*, in the South African war, went to Cape Town in 1901; and the *Ocean Ranger* lived up to her name in 1878 by voyaging not only to Cape Province and Natal but to Mauritius and across the Indian Ocean to Port Adelaide, South Australia and even, it appears, on to New Zealand — further from her home port than any other Fowey ship I can trace.

The steamships were far from being the only competition. While Britain's steam tonnage had doubled that of the rest of the world, the Americans especially had improved the efficiency of sail beyond the ken of many a West country owner as, for example, when the 2,556-ton *Rebecca Palmer* of Boston, on her maiden voyage, came into Fowey on July 15 1901 for 1,500 tons of china clay.

The first five-mast schooner to cross the Atlantic, 296 feet in length, she was at the time the largest sailing vessel to have entered the port. At Fowey her visit aroused much comment. The shops expected lively business as informed opinion declared her crew to be some forty hands. In fact, it was ten — no more than some local vessels that were dwarfed alongside her. (For example the 207-ton *Waterwitch* of Portsmouth, later of Fowey, had a crew of eight in summer, ten in winter). All the *Rebecca Palmer*'s heavy work (lifting sails, *etc.*) was done by steam power. In 1907 she paid her shareholders 27%.

THE 'LITTLE' SHIPS AND NEWFOUNDLAND

However, it was their very smallness (plus, relative to the Americans, their crews' low pay) that enabled some Fowey vessels at this period still to earn a living on blue water. This was the justification for John Stephens's fleet of *Littles*. Small tonnage, shallow draught vessels could enter havens denied to larger ones and could often avoid lighterage and other charges. They could get in and out more readily, did not have to await high water, could go alongside where others could not, could navigate shallows more easily. Their manoeuvrability gave them quicker turn-round at lower cost so long as there were cargoes or part cargoes to be had at difficult points of shipment, such as there were prior to their being connected by road and rail transport with larger, better provided, better served ports, harbours, docks and quays.

Despite having the only deep-water harbour between Plymouth and Falmouth, with anchorage for draughts of eighteen feet, Fowey never seems to have had much luck with vessels much larger than 300 tons. Also the sub-ports of Mevagissey, Pentewan, Charlestown, Par, Polperro and Looe were all capable of taking small vessels only. So, with few exceptions who found employment elsewhere, Fowey masters had always been born and bred to small ships.

It may have been this predilection for smallness that kept the port's ships for so long in some deep water trades. In Newfoundland, with a coast lacerated with elongated inlets sheltering communities living off the world's richest fishery, little ships could pick up a few tons from a village here, a few tons from a township there, so making up a cargo for Europe, South America or the West Indies. And in this trade Fowey continued (though in a much restricted way) right down to the 1920s, long after (for instance) Poole, whose prosperity was founded on it, had totally given it up — in about the 1860s.

55 The fast-sailing little *Isabella*, 61 tons, built by Gibbs at Galmpton, Dartmouth 1864. Under the management of several Fowey master mariners — James Allen Tippett from 1865, William Arthur Wyatt in 1886 and Charles Swiggs in 1890 — she was mainly a coaster but went occasionally on deep-water. Acquiring her in 1893, John Stephens put her into the Newfoundland trade. Her sharp-floored hull performed exceptionally well on deep water but was the death of her in the shallows of St. John's in 1913. When 'she touched ground — she topelled over'.

National Maritime Museum

Various local owners had ships engaged in it in the second part of the 19th century — Luke, Hicks, Couch, Rillston, Tadd, Hocken and others — though by the 1890s, the principal one was probably Stephens. All Stephens's 10 *Littles* but one were in it in all but the winter months, hard driven, often under stun'sails, to and fro across the Western Ocean. Also there was the smallest, without the prefix — *Isabella*, acquired in 1893 when thirty years old, repaired, re-rigged with square yards at the fore, with topmast and lower stun'sails. She ran for twenty years in the trade with a crew of four, 61 gross tons, carrying only 80 tons of cargo. No vessel in the trade did such fast voyages with such consistency. Yet the *Isabella* was not the smallest so employed; this was probably the *Florrie*, a Bideford ketch of 46 tons, that Mr. Robert S. Munn recalled in *Sea Breezes* in June

1933 as visiting Harbour Grace in 1889. And there were others almost as small.

The Newfoundland trade is well documented, as becomes one of such ancient lineage, by Dr. Basil Greenhill in his *The Merchant Schooners*, in many other works including Basil Lubbock's classics, and, so far as Stephens are concerned, in my monographs on that fleet and the *Isabella*. If because of this it is considered unnecessary to say more about it here, that should not be taken as meaning that it had less than major importance for the ships of the port of Fowey. Newfoundland salted cod took them across deep water probably more than any other cargo.

It has also been pointed out that small vessels had an advantage in the then notorious shallows of the Rio de la Plata, with its access to Montevideo, Rosario, Buenos Aires and other places on the Plata—Panama—Paraguay river system — 'There vessels of greater draught than 13 feet or so had to stand offshore and offload to lighters and keels not always there when wanted and addicted to overcharging and other scandalous tricks. A cost-saving master, refusing a pilot, could easily get stuck in mud for months till the melting of the winter snows inland raised the river level'.

FISHING VESSELS

By the last years of the 19th century the concern of Mevagissey, Looe and Polperro with cargo carrying had declined to a low level, their labour and capital being taken up almost entirely with their fishing. Par, Charlestown and Pentewan shared the carrying trade with Fowey harbour, though Pentewan had to put up a continual struggle against silting, for which it had been notorious since it had been built in the late 1820s. Commercially, it faded out after 1914.

The present monograph is concerned with merchant ships and only incidentally with fishing vessels, yet fishing is relevant for various reasons. In the earlier part of the period we have dealt with, small vessels were often used, according to circumstances, for both cargo carrying and fishing. Nets, tackle, barrel staves, salt and other requirements for fishing all had to be imported, as did the timber for its boats, almost all built in local yards. Fishing was a major alternative to, as well as part of, seafaring. So its relative importance, its distribution throughout the port, need to be considered.

In 1886, Mevagissey landed a larger quantity of fish than any other place in the West country — 255,000 cwt to a value of £211,000 (Brixham 48,000 and Plymouth 142,000). St. Ives was the next biggest in Cornwall with 102,000 cwt. These compared nationally with the largest, Grimsby, with 1,384,000 cwt. Looe landed 18,000 cwt and Polperro 9,000 cwt.

Unlike Mevagissey, fishing out of Fowey harbour was never important, possibly due to the lack of landing facilities. The railway, when it arrived in 1869, constructed a fish quay on the west bank, and in 1883

56 Pentewan tidal basin about 1900; built about 1825 with some 300 yards of quayage as a point of shipment alternative to Charlestown. It was linked by mineral railway with St. Austell, but the sand dried for a cable's length outside its entrance and its continued silting up caused vessels to shun it for fear of being neaped.

Wheal Martyn China Clay Museum, St. Austell

57, 58 Mevagissey, two harbour scenes of which are seen here in the early 1900s, had twice the population of Fowey in the 18th century, by the end of which much of it had been rebuilt from the proceeds of its pilchard fishery and smuggling.

Mevagissey & District Museum Society

the Brazen Island Sardine Company Ltd. built a factory at Polruan in the expectation that it would revive pilchard fishing. But neither had much lasting influence, and the sardine factory closed about 1914. More permanent was salmon fishing, described in the 1880s as, along with seafaring, the main occupation of the inhabitants of Polruan, who had four salmon seines on the river pre-1914.

The Merchant Shipping Act of 1894 required fishing boats to be registered, and the first volume of the Fowey Custom House Sea Fishing Boat Register, from May 12 1902 to December 24 1907 contains particulars of some 200 boats. As well as such information as each boat's name, number, rig and measurements, it records the name of the owner and the place to which it belongs. From it, one may arrive at some indication of

59 Traverse board incised on the bellows of the fishing vessel *Maggie* (FY22). The traverse board was an ancient and approximate means of recording the courses run during a watch. The holes and stringed pegs enable the course traversed to be indicated.

Tesseract, Hastings-on-Hudson, New York

the relative extent of commercial fishing in the various places within the port:

70 boats belonged to Mevagissey
57 boats belonged to Looe
43 boats belonged to Gorran Haven
12 boats belonged to Polperro
 8 boats belonged to Polruan
 5 boats belonged to Fowey
 4 boats belonged to Par
 1 boat belonged to Portmellon
 1 boat belonged to Portloe.

The Act provided for each boat to bear the letters (in Fowey's case FY) and number assigned to it. It excluded from registration boats navigated by oars only.

THE YACHT BUILDERS

The construction of boats for the fishery became an even more important source of income for yards that no longer built schooners and other cargo carriers. Aside from this and their repair work, they became widely reputed in the palmy days before 1914 for their yachts and other pleasure craft, into which went materials and craftsmanship of a high order. Indeed the late Victorian and Edwardian expansion of yachting locally, especially at Fowey itself, which was almost ideally placed for it, attracted boatwrights to the locality from other centres, where the decline of shipbuilding had been just as sharp and the market for pleasure craft considerably less.

New names came to supplement those of the remaining schooner builders of the century's last years — Slade and Butson at Fowey, Shapcott at Looe, Tregaskes at Par and Roberts at Mevagissey.

This new generation of builders of boats and yachts that arrived with the 1880s were: at Fowey, William H. Watty and John Clemens, (the latter from Gannel, Newquay, where his family — as Y & J Clemens — had built schooners from 1834—1881, including Fowey's *Mary Peers*), also Richard Heller; at Mevagissey, Frazier Brothers and Richard Pill (Gorran); and at Looe, Peter Ferris, Thomas Pearce and James Angear.

The earliest beginnings of pleasure boating and sailing in the port are lost in the sea mists of time. The recreational amenities of Looe, at least, were well on the map by 1800 when the *Sherborne Mercury* advertised 'a new bathing machine on a fine sandy beach' there. At Fowey, rowing regattas were an annual event probably much earlier than 1835 when that year's was described in the *Royal Cornwall Gazette*.

Local sailing for pleasure seems to date significantly from the third quarter of the century, though its growth depended in part on visitors; and Fowey's Collector of Customs, Emra Holmes, writing in the Christmas number of the *Masonic Magazine*, deplored the shortage of accommodation there — 'apart from the old Ship Inn and the modern Commercial Inn there is no place where visitors can stay, except two or three very comfortable, though small, lodging houses on the Esplanade'.

However, what later came to be called tourism was encouraged by the Great Western Railway's promotion of the idea of a Cornish Riviera, in rivalry to the fashionable South of France variety, served by a different line. The approaches to the region were improved by, for instance, the opening of the Lostwithiel—Fowey railway to passengers in 1883. In 1882 the Fowey Hotel was established. And similar developments at Looe, and elsewhere, eased the way for visitors, though by present-day standards they were a mere trickle and confined to the well-to-do.

So by the 1890s recreative sailing and boating for both residents and visitors were well established, and in 1894 the Fowey Yacht Club was built where John Stephens had launched schooners twenty years earlier. Ten years later the mooring of the Royal yacht *Osborne* was rewarded by a letter of thanks from her captain, and from 1905 Fowey's Yacht Club became 'Royal'. In the 1880s yachts were built on the Yacht Club site, the last one being the 18-ton cutter yacht, *Airy-Mouse*, (March 1894) by W.H. Watty.

One notable yachtsman of those days was Mr. Charles Ebenezer Treffry (1840—1924) of Place, Fowey, whose steam yachts were a local feature. He bought his first in 1881, the 19-ton *Udney*, and sold her to two Dartmouth engineers two years later. In 1889 he acquired the 22-ton steel yacht *Busy Bee*, bought in 1896 from him by the Marine Biological Association at Plymouth. In 1905 he bought the 68-ton *Sparkle* selling her to Belgium seven years later. But his still-remembered yacht was the *Twinkle*, 31 tons, bought in 1913 and sold in 1923. She remained on the register until 1943 when she was acquired by the Ministry of War Transport.

Apart from the steam yachts *Udney* and *Busy Bee*, I can detect little in the way of pleasure craft on the register prior to 1890, but then yachts of less, as well as of more, than the statutory 15 tons began to appear, possibly to safeguard the owner's title when going foreign. The number owned by non-residents also grew with the passing of time.

MOTOR CRAFT

Mr. Treffry's steam yachts were all built elsewhere, but the internal combustion engine was more suitable than steam for the small craft that were within local builders' capabilities, and others began to follow the fashion set locally by Henry Roberts' *Skirmish* in 1902, already described. Also owners of the smaller registered sailing vessels began to have them fitted with auxiliary, petrol-fuelled, internal combustion motors, capable of 5—8 knots.

In 1909 Thomas Oliver of Polperro had a 15-horse-power motor installed in his 17-ton dandy-rigged *Alarm*. The same year, the cutter yacht *Foye*, built at Gorran Haven five years previously, was fortified by 'one inverted petrol motor of unknown date and make', yielding 7½ knots. And in 1911, Henry Paull of the Fowey Tug and Salvage Company had his 18-ton ketch *Rival* converted into a motor cutter.

Yet, despite the publicity given to international motor boat competitions, the success of participants and the establishment of the magazine *Motor Boat* in 1904, the new means of propulsion was suspect and its progress tortuous other than for pleasure. In 1907 the Fowey Harbour Commissioners declined 'for the present' to license motor boats until Board of Trade guidance had been obtained. Also although the inadequacy of the oared ferry service between Polruan and Fowey had long been complained of, it was not until 1912 that a motor boat was introduced for the purpose. And then the licensed watermen objected to its being used for pleasure trips.....No doubt similar difficulties arose elsewhere.

In those pulling boat days, by the way, the lesser business of the port involved a much greater number of small craft than subsequently, after the application more generally of mechanical power both afloat and ashore had enabled more work to be done, faster and with less physical effort. In 1904 the Fowey Harbour Commissioners licensed as many as 93 watermen and 135 boats.

EFFECTS OF WORLD WAR I

Wind-power alone continued to be the predominant, if declining, means of propulsion until after World War I when it was given new life in the short sea trades by auxiliary motors of one kind or another. The quinquennial list of Fowey-registered ships at the end of 1910 returned 68 sailing vessels (7,468 tons) and 11 steam (1,922 tons). Under 'Steam' were included the cargo carriers *Deerhound*, *Torfrey*, *Par* and *Foy*; the tugs *Treffry*, *Countess of Jersey* and *Gallant*; also the yachts *Sparkle*, *Foye*, *Alarm* and *Skirmish*, the last three in fact being petrol motor powered.

Of the 68 sailing vessels at the end of 1910 some 13 were certainly pleasure craft from their registered particulars, so that the tally of the port's sailing merchantmen was about 55.

Compared with a total of 79 registered ships in 1910, there were, by 1920, only 39 (my own estimate in lieu of an official list for that year). The cargo steamship *Foy* and the three tugs had survived, and there was now the steam yacht *Twinkle*. Of sailing vessels there were 34, and that included 11 yachts and a lighter, so that

immediately post-war there were some 22 sailing merchantmen and of these at least five had been acquired since 1916 mainly as replacements for losses. The outbreak of war on August 4 1914 paralysed the freight market but, from November, rates began to rise and soon it became apparent that ships in whatever condition were a good investment. Requisitioning drove freights up further, the shortage of shipping space worsened. Naval reservists were called up, crews became hard to get. Germany answered the Allied

60 Built as a brig at Milford, Pembroke, in 1873, the *Martha Edmonds* was transferred from Llanelly to Fowey five years later on being bought by James Clunes, Par merchant, and Edward Rillston, Fowey grocer and draper.

They had her salted and yellow-metalled. Rillston took over management from Clunes in 1886 but two years later relinquished control to Edward Stephens who had her re-rigged as a three-mast schooner. She sailed on deep water

for only a few years and spent most of her life coasting till 1915 when she was torpedoed and sunk.

Sotheby's, Belgravia

blockade with submarines, and war risk insurance for shipping was taken over by the Government. In 1915 the U-boat menace began to take effect after Germany declared all enemy merchant ships liable to attack when in waters around the British Isles. Merchantmen had to be armed, and for their defence, 12-pounders were mounted aft to aid vessels' escape. But Fowey's kind of small sailing craft were really sitting ducks.

The first casualty was the once foreign-going, three-mast, 176-ton schooner *Frau Minna Petersen*, built at Portmadoc in 1878, named for the wife of a German merchant from whom it was hoped to get charters. Bought in 1901 by Captain Robert May, a Par master mariner, she was captured two days after the declaration of war and taken into Emden as a prize, then sold to a German subject in November. May put her value at the time at £1,500 (upwards of £30,000 at current values). 'I've lost all my possessions', he said, 'my entire capital was locked up in the ship'.

61 The *Katie Cluett*, second of four vessels built by John Stephens in Whitford's Yard, Fowey, 1874—1878. Her first owner was John Clark Isaac, a Liskeard merchant who ran her out of Looe, especially to the South Wales ports. She rivalled the *Rhoda Mary* of Falmouth as the fastest coasting schooner of her day.
National Maritime Museum

Of Toyne Carter's fine fleet of six steamers, four survived hostilities to be sold elsewhere, two having been lost previously, but war all but finished off the sailers. Those that did escape the U-boat were little more than viable survivors of what, by the 1920s, was another age.

Stephens were severe sufferers. In sixteen months they lost eleven vessels by enemy action and the fleet would have ceased to exist by the end of hostilities had it not been for the hurried acquisition of replacements. All the *Littles* by then were memories.

A loss, though not from enemy action, that hit local families badly was that of the 256-ton barquentine *Ada Peard*, built for the Hocken family at Par in 1875 as a general deep-sea trader. She was wrecked at Salmon River, Nova Scotia, September 2 1916. That terminated her registry at Fowey where she had lately been acquired by the Slade family of shipbuilders, Ernest Congden Slade her managing owner.

However, it must be assumed that she was made seaworthy. On December 23 1916 she was re-registered at Halifax by the Minister of Marine and Fisheries as owned by a Gladys Irene Gibson of that city. In January, she passed to three St. John's, Newfoundland merchants — George M. Barr, Walter Stanley Munroe and Arthur S. Rendell. She went on the St. John's register a year later.

In November 1916, Messrs. Munroe and Rendell also acquired the other Hocken barquentine — the *E.S. Hocken*, Fowey's biggest sailer. But a year later she too was lost — abandoned on December 15 1917 in the North Atlantic, 23.25N 48.17W, and set on fire to prevent her being taken by the enemy.

Other than those already mentioned, casualties were, from enemy action: the barquentines Stephens's *Ocean Swell* and Kellow's *Maria*; also the schooners *Silvia, Conoid, Perseverance, Spin-away, Bessie Stephens, Martha Edmonds, Harriet Williams, Little Mystery, Little Gem* and *Jessie*. Lost to their owners from other causes during the war were the Whitstable-owned 266-ton barquentine *Ruby*, a collier; and the schooners *Sarah Ann, Ocean Wave, Katie Cluett* and *Little Secret*.

62 The brigantine *Adelaide*, S. Bate master, A.E. Benney owner, painted by Chappell before she was altered to a schooner in 1917. Built at Padstow in 1869 for the Fowey merchants, Albertus and William Warren Dingle, she had various managers before Benney transferred her to Falmouth in 1924: Richard Prior Toms from 1877, John Merryfield from 1883, Charles Morris from 1890 and Inkerman Tregaskes from 1896.

Mr. N. Purdie, Holmbush, St. Austell

EARLIER LOSSES

The port lost some 20 ships in these war years yet that average, of five per annum, was not a great deal more than average annual losses over the whole 153 years from 1786—1939 — 3.50 vessels a year. The losses in 1917 were exceeded only by the number of those in 1808 (14, including 5 seizures). Other bad years were 1805 (12, including 10 seizures) and 1807 (12, including 7 seizures), also 10 in each of 1881*, 1885 and 1887*. Others were: 9 in each of 1806 (5 seizures), 1864, 1878; 8 in each of 1816 (3 seizures), 1882*, 1891* and 1896; 7 in each of 1855, 1859, 1866, 1869, 1871, 1890, 1902 and 1911. (Years with an asterisk were of especially heavy gales in home waters).

Of all the ships registered over the 153 years, 540 are recorded as having been lost to their owners by wrecking, sinking, foundering, abandonment, seizure, capture or unknown cause. The dates of 39 of them are unstated, including four taken by the enemy. Before 1815 the dates of losses to the enemy were recorded only exceptionally.

WHAT WERE LEFT

Where Fowey's gross tonnage of ships in 1910 had been 16,134, by 1920 it had collapsed to 3,564, never to recover.

At December 31 1920 the following 49 ships, (for port numbers and years of registration see Index), were what were left:

13 schooners — *Thomas Aylan, Lizzie Trenberth, Adelaide, Jane Slade, Florence, Lydia Cardell, Pedestrian, Amy, Helena Anna, Jane Banks, Traveller, Earl Cairns, Trevellas;*
7 ketches — *Lizzie, Beatrice Caroline, Industry, G.H. Bevan, W.E. Gladstone, Isabel, Rival;*
1 barquentine — *Waterwitch;*
1 brigantine — *Raymond;*
1 sloop — *Richard & Jane;*
1 lighter — *Titania;*

5 steamers — *Treffry, Countess of Jersey, Gallant, Foy, Twinkle* (steam yacht*);
10 yachts* — *Foam, Otter, Theodora, Water Witch, Rosemary, Skirmish, Foye, Fancy, Marjorie, Little Pal.*

*Craft used for pleasure, not plying for hire. All 11 averaged only 13 tons.

The brigantine *Raymond*, 200 tons, built on Prince Edward Island in 1876, had been transferred to Fowey from Faversham in 1916 by her Poole owners, who employed her in the home trade. She survived the 1914—1918 war to become a moored training ship in the Thames. A London merchant, Charles James Quirk, bought her in 1929, re-named her *Lady Quirk*, and transferred her to Douglas, IOM. Broken up in World War II, she was the last of the British-owned, PEI-built vessels.

63 The ketch *Rival*, last merchantman under sail to be built (1889) in the port of Fowey. *National Maritime Museum*

CHAPTER FIVE

MERCHANT SAIL'S SUCCESSORS MOTOR SHIPS AND YACHTS 1921–1939

During the war freight rates had rocketed, and from about 1916 even vessels in their dotage were being bought at prices five to ten times more than those of two years previously. Ships made profits as never before, and shipping companies mushroomed.

Yet by the end of 1919, although world shipbuilding capacity had been so increased that all war losses had been made good, the euphoria of peace was such that few people realised they were about to be glutted by cargo space, that big profits were to become big losses.

The account that follows of one Fowey-bought vessel exemplifies the hazards of the period.

The shipbroking firm of Toyne, Carter and Company was founded in 1896 when John Peers Carter (1872–1957), lately of Connah's Quay on the Chester River, went into partnership with Charles Louis Toyne (ca 1870–1921), ship's husband of Fowey. They initiated the port's major steamship venture, already referred to, and soon became one of its two leading shipbrokers and agents.

THE 'A.B. SHERMAN'

On September 21 1919 they bought the 3-mast schooner A.B. Sherman of Philadelphia from the US Consul at Plymouth acting on behalf of the American owners. She had been built at Boston, Massachusetts, in 1883 and employed mainly in the coal trade from Virginia. Not long before the United States declared war on Germany in April 1917, she had been seized off the Scillies supplying a U-boat, then taken to Plymouth as a prize and stripped down in Devonport Dockyard.

Her new owners had her towed to Fowey where she was laid up in Pont Pill, and arrangements were made for J. Slade & Sons to rebuild and refit her. She was too big for their yard so the work was done *in situ*. For use as a workshop they re-erected a 60-foot army surplus hut beside Pont Pill, subsequently the home of the novelist Leo Walmsley.

The work took longer than expected. She had been shell-holed on one side by her captor and on the other by the submarine attempting to forestall her capture. Also her foremast had been damaged by a bomb placed against it, under-deck. Holed topsides only, she might have been put to sea quickly with new foremast and some patching, but her owners wanted a Lloyd's classification for her, and Slade's found it no easy task to satisfy the surveyors.

Meanwhile what had been an acute shortage of ships when she had been bought was fast becoming a surplus.

She was refitted as a 4-master. Her running bowsprit

64 At Pensacola under her original colours, the US schooner A.B. Sherman (Captain W. Grace) c. 1916. Built as a three-master in Boston in 1883, 167.7 ft in length, 581 net tons, she was mainly in the coal and timber trades until acquired at Fowey.

Courtesy of Pensacola Historical Society

65 The A.B. Sherman after re-building to a four-master in 1920/1921 by Slade's. Bought in September 1919 by Toyne, Carter & Co. and registered at Fowey October 13 1921, she was the second largest sailing vessel to belong to the port, exceeded only by the Bangalore of 1857, 760 tons. She was sold foreign 1923.

66 The *Earl Cairns*, built at Connah's Quay, Flint, 1883, bought by Toyne, Carter & Co., 1917. Acquired by a Gloucester owner in 1924, she suffered an engine room fire that caused her abandonment to the underwriters in 1929. Again certified seaworthy, she was re-registered and bought by Frederick Samuel Harris of Appledore who transferred her to Bideford. She finished her days at Falmouth after barrage balloon duties.

was dispensed with to save retracting it and slacking up her stays while in port. Under the main keel she was given a false one about nine inches deep. The centre-box-with-plate that she had had when built was taken away to keelson level. Each of her outside pitch pine planks was 42 feet x 8" x 5", weighing 2½ cwt, and either side from deck to waterline amidships fifteen of them were renewed. And much other work was done, so that she stretched Slade's capabilities to the limit.

After about eighteen months' labour she was completed in the autumn of 1921 and registered at Fowey October 13. Re-numbered 131,989, KJWF, she measured 623 tons gross, 177.7x35.5x15 feet, and classed 'A' for six years by special survey December 1921.

But by the time she was fit for sea, trade had shrunk and there was a glut of ships and few cargoes. She had cost £16,627 and £6,535 had been spent on her, yet in November 1921 she was valued independently at £1,100.

Worse was to come. In the spring of 1922, arriving at Leghorn with china clay, water was found to have got into her cargo. In serious difficulties, she had to be sold to Italians. She realised £500!

In England her register was closed in November 1923. She had traded on Toyne, Carter's account for only a few months. Refitted, she had cost them £23,162, while her losses on voyage account were £25,000. She had put her owners out of pocket by some £48,000!

The *A.B. Sherman* was Fowey's second largest sailer, exceeded only by the 760-ton barque *Bangalore* of 1857, another big-ship tragedy as I have pointed out earlier.

THE 'EARL CAIRNS'

Two other schooners had been acquired by Toyne, Carter in these fast-changing years — the *Earl Cairns* in 1917, built at Connah's Quay in 1884, 127 tons; and the *Mary Peers* in 1921, twenty tons bigger, an auxiliary motor screw vessel then nearly fifty years old. Two years later she was stranded, a total loss.

The *Earl Cairns* was fitted with an auxiliary motor screw in 1921 and continued successfully in the coasting trade, mainly with china clay till May 1929, when she had a fire in her engine room, was a constructive loss and had to be abandoned to the underwriters. But in the November, she was given a certificate of seaworthiness and acquired by Frederick Samuel Harris, an Appledore owner who transferred her to Bideford.

Some idea of the costs involved in operating a Fowey coaster at this period may be gained from the *Earl Cairns* running costs. Between January 19 and October 30 1923 she traded: Weymouth — Guernsey — Plymouth — Looe — Fowey — Plymouth — Rouen — Poole — Rouen — Dieppe — Teignmouth — Rosslare — Glasgow — Dunkirk — Rochester — Grangemouth — London — Par — Weston Point — Fowey — Par. Her disbursements on port charges amounted to £284.

Per month wages totalled £39.50 (master £12; mate £7.50; engineer £9; cook £6; AB £5) and victuals £16.87 (11.25d per man per day for 30 days). Insurance was £5.50. Per month, in addition was oil at £21; and wear, tear and maintenance, estimated at £12 but in the event £23. Her estimated monthly operating cost of £91 was, in fact, nearer £117.

Another late war acquisition was by Ernest Congden Slade in 1918 of the 127-ton, 3-master *Trevellas*. She had been launched fully-rigged from the foreshore at St. Agnes forty-two years previously and had spent much of her time as a coaster between the Bristol Channel and Ireland. The Kearons and Tyrrells, master mariners of Arklow, soon bought her and transferred her to Dublin in 1929.

THE 'WATERWITCH'

Urgently scouring the ports for a successor to his barquentine the *Ocean Swell*, sunk by U-boat off the Start on July 5 1917, Edward Stephens lit upon the derelict of a vessel that, deep laden with coal in 1916, had had to run for Newlyn harbour in a south-easter and struck bottom, damaged below by impact and above by fire. She was the barquentine *Waterwitch*, usually driven so hard that she was known as the 'Portsmouth workhouse' among seamen. Lifted to a berth to clear the fairway, she was for breaking up and tenders were sought. Stephens bought both her and her cargo, had her patched, pumped, floated and towed to Par in May 1918. There, having sold her cargo, he had her rebuilt by Tregaskes, whose work on her enabled her to trade with distinction for another seventeen years under Stephens's flag.

67 *Waterwitch*: on deck looking forward in the Channel, Fowey—Newcastle, April 1930.

Subsequently one of the best known vessels in the mercantile marine, she had been built as a brig by Thomas Meadus at Poole in 1871 and altered to a barquentine in 1884. Her durability has been attributed in part to century-seasoned oak from Portsmouth Dockyard being used in her frames, timber no longer

68 *Waterwitch* bound for the Gulf of Finland and new owners, getting under way from Par for the last time, spring 1939.

needed for iron warships. Planked with pitch pine and copper fastened, she was 207 tons gross and 112 feet long. Captain Charles Deacon of Charlestown was appointed her master, serving her for sixteen years. She was paired with Stephens's 3-mast schooner, the *Lydia Cardell* under Deacon's brother-in-law George Beynon, which had been bought in 1919 from the Tyrrells of Arklow. She was another old-timer, launched at Appledore in 1873, one-time trader to North America, the West Indies and the Mediterranean.

Making a trio with the *Waterwitch* and the *Lydia Cardell* was another 3-mast schooner, the *Frau Minna Peterson*, returned by Germany to the Red Ensign in 1919. Edward Stephens became her managing owner for the Shipping Controller in the December and she was once again registered at Fowey, but this time as the *Jane Banks*, after Stephens's mother.

Another prize-of-war was the steel, 3-mast schooner *S.F. Pearce*, formerly *Weser* and *Marie Linnemann* under the German flag. She had been built in 1908 at Hammelwarden, 213 tons, and was bought by Samuel Pearce, master mariner of Pentewan and registered at Fowey in May 1924. He had an auxiliary motor installed in 1928 and employed her as a china clay coaster.

These, then, were the port's main acquisitions as war turned to peace. Their cargoes were chiefly china clay, china stone and coal, increasingly difficult to find as the 1920s passed.

THE POST-WAR SCENE

From its inception as a raw material in 1755, English china clay had been regarded by consumers worldwide as superior to any produced elsewhere, and by 1914 output had risen to a peak. But disorganised sea transport in the war made dependable export deliveries impossible, causing other countries to develop their own deposits behind tariff and other barriers. Steady progress pre-war was checked, export markets were lost, and production between 1919 and 1939 made little increase and, even then, only because of growing home consumption. Throughout this period the competition of vessels registered elsewhere, particularly abroad, became more and more acute so that china clay freights yielded a negligible return (if any) for the few ships still owned locally.

69 Barquentine *Waterwitch*: up in the bows 1930/1931, two oil paintings by Arthur Bradbury ARWA (1892—1977), as are 71, 74 and 75.

70 *Waterwitch*: on deck looking aft (a) starboard side, 1931, Liverpool; (b) port side, 1930.

71 *Waterwitch*: below deck, April 1930 (a) fo'castle; (b) cabin.

Along with much else, the whole Cornish scene had changed since the Great Divide of the European war as it was first called. As I summarised in my monograph on Stephens's ships, and I can do no better here, 'seine fishing had been abandoned — in 1925 — and the pilchard shoals no longer provided the proverbial meat, money and light. What was left of the mines had boomed during hostilities only to collapse afterwards. Miners who had not emigrated formed choirs and sang for pennies. The Newfoundland trade that had dropped in the war never revived after it. The heavy, horse-drawn wagons that by the score trundled the china clay and stone from the kilns down to the harbours and railway trucks were replaced by motor lorries. Clay that wasn't bulk-loaded down chutes into ships' holds was packed in paper bags that had largely replaced casks; the war had cut off the supply of barrel staves. More and more cargoes that had gone coastwise by ship were being carried not only by rail but by road, on which hundreds of ex-WD motor lorries now plied and new ones too'.

Harbours and their installations had been starved of repairs and maintenance, loading facilities were so inadequate that ships refused to come, turn-round time was excessive, dredging had been so neglected that vessels went aground. It took at least ten to fifteen years for the backlog to be worked off, and it was done largely under the direction of Captain Fred Collins R.N., D.S.C., appointed Fowey's Harbour Master in 1919.

In 1921 a dozen steamers and sailers were laid up in Fowey harbour alone, more by 1925. In the 1920s imports virtually ceased with the exception of coal — steam coal from South Wales and other kinds from the north-east coast and the Chester river. No longer were staves needed for china clay and pilchard casks. The imports from Plymouth of limestone for the kilns at the heads of creeks ceased about 1929 after a long decline, burnt limestone for sweetening Cornwall's acid soil being replaced by the ground variety and other fertilisers. Roadstone no longer came by sea but by lorry. Salt, that pre-war came from Cadiz, had disappeared with the pilchard export trade. Even supplies for the grocers' and other shops, which had long been brought from Plymouth in the ketch *Rival*, finished by 1926 when she was succeeded by the motor lorry and sold foreign. She had been bought in 1920 by

a Plymouth provision merchant. Her former owner, Henry Paull of the Fowey Tug & Salvage Company died in the autumn of 1924.

SIR ARTHUR QUILLER-COUCH

When in 1925 Sir Arthur Quiller-Couch (1863—1944) resigned as chairman of Fowey's Harbour Commissioners after twenty-one years, the port's shipping community began to lose the guidance of the most notable Cornishman of his day. Also a Trinity House Pilotage sub-commissioner, he had a reputation among local shipping people that was overlaid by his wider fame as author and scholar, Professor of English Literature at Cambridge.

Very much the local boy, he was grandson of Dr. Jonathan Couch, physician and naturalist, Polperro's historian. 'Q' was an incisive maritime critic, a martinet indeed, who had little reverence for august authority, and was the first person to draw public attention to the menace of coastal oil pollution.

In a long letter to the *Times* of January 16 1920 he recalled that in the war, cargo vessels were instructed to fetch home urgently-needed fuel oil in their tanks in place of water ballast. Because skippers disobeyed orders, docks got contaminated. 'Land-locked Fowey', he said, 'where shipping pays dues on 300,000 tons a year, suffered from stench, slime and pollution for miles of foreshore. Concurrently, the fish deserted the Fowey estuary, at a time when food was scarce'.

From May 17 1918 representations had been made to Government Ministries urging action, but the correspondence and relevant orders from them were a 'revelation of official blunder, dilatoriness and evasion'. Of the Ministry of Shipping he wrote: 'So the Great War is over, but this Government department still runs on; and so, at frequent intervals, does the flood of filth into our poor little harbour'.

It had been 'Q' too who, as early as 1898, had pressed for the intelligent development of his Delectable Duchy for holidays. 'Were it within human capacity to decide between a revival of our ancient industries, fishery and mining, and the development of new business, our decision would be prompt enough. But it is not. Well then, since we must cater for the stranger, let us do it well and honestly. Let us respect him and our native land as well'. Before he died he was to witness a massive expansion in Cornwall's income from holiday-making, retirement and recreation, and to see the

72 The auxiliary motor schooner *Rigdin*, 397 tons, launched in Finland in 1907 as *Ingrid*, a fine ship that had traded under Finnish, Russian and British colours before being laid up at Southampton. Having lost the *Lydia Cardell*, Edward Stephens bought her in 1929 to fulfil a coal contract to Falmouth gasworks, found to be too large for the purpose, she was laid up after only a few months. Broken up at Plymouth 1939.

National Maritime Museum

pleasure craft belonging to his Fowey far outnumber the mercantile, outward symbols of a more leisured, though not more leisurely, age.

THE LAST ACQUISITIONS UNDER SAIL

In March 1929 Stephens's Company of Little Ships, as it had been known in its palmier days, suffered its last disaster. The *Lydia Cardell*, with silver sand, Rouen — Sunderland, was run down by a steamer off Flamborough Head, a total loss. She represented more than a third of the owners' carrying capacity and they had an important contract to deliver coal for the Falmouth gasworks. She was replaced by the biggest ship they had ever owned — the 397-ton auxiliary motor schooner *Rigdin*, once called *Ingrid*, a Finnish-built vessel that had been idle for six-and-a-half years. It proved a tragic mistake.

The *Rigdin* was acquired in September 1929, just one month before the collapse of the American stock market plunged the world into depression. Moreover, her draught was found to be much too great for coasting and there were such other deficiencies that it is a matter for speculation as to how she came to be bought at all. She was totally unsuitable for the purpose, never went to Falmouth and made her last voyage in March 1931 before being laid up in Pont Pill. After eight years there, she was towed to Plymouth and

broken up — yet another of Fowey's big-ship tragedies. She was never transferred from the Southampton register.

Even in the mid-thirties, she was not the last local acquisition under sail. This was the 3-mast schooner *Mary Miller*, 119 tons, built at Carrickfergus in 1881, and bought at the end of 1934 by Charles Phillips Couch, the Pentewan shipbroker. China clay was then recovering from the depression. After a record tonnage in 1927 output had dropped by 40% by 1932. The leading firms in it then merged to form the English China Clay Group that has led the industry ever since, and over the next five years production climbed back.

It was not until 1940 that the *Mary Miller* had twin screw motors fitted, and she served as a single-masted barge at Greenock before being laid up at Par, the last Fowey schooner to trade. Strictly speaking, the *Katie*, usually credited with the distinction of being the last engineless schooner to trade from a UK port, belonged to Padstow where she was built in 1881 although owned by Clunes & Company of Par.

It was during the depression that there appeared in some numbers the Dutch type of motor coaster, very familiar since, that was perhaps the ultimate finish of the few remaining china clay carriers under sail, assisted mechanically or not. It had been developed in

Holland from the *Schuyt* for estuaries, rivers and canals, of shallow draught, with engines and accommodation aft, big hold and electrical gear. It was admirably suited to china clay out of Par and Charlestown where harbour dues and other costs were lighter than in deep-watered Fowey. So where, between 1930 and 1938, the number of clay-laden vessels leaving Fowey harbour remained more or less static, the count out of Par and Charlestown grew by 60%.

FOWEY'S SHIPS — 1935

By December 31 1935 motor vessels ('propelled by mechanical power other than steam') had been made a distinct category in the official return of ships registered at Fowey. Of these there were 34, but at least 31 of them were yachts. Only one was a motor auxiliary merchantman, the schooner *S.F. Pearce*.

The only unassisted sailers were: Stephens's *Jane Banks* and *Waterwitch*; Couch's *Mary Miller*; the *Thomas Aylan*, Fowey-built in 1860, the oldest vessel on the register, owned by a Liverpool barge and tug proprietor; and Kellow's *Helena Anna*. Captain William Varcoe Kellow, the Pentewan shipbroker, had bought the 3-mast schooner *Helena Anna* in 1893, 179 tons, built in 1870 by Axel Drenth at Pekela, Holland. She was an old deep-sea trader that had transferred to coasting but was now, in 1935, laid up in Fowey harbour.

By this time the 'Sailing vessel' category in the official return had been demoted to being a mere repository for everything other than motor and steam ships. It included harbour craft — dredgers, barges, etc. — these having been required by the 1921 Merchant Shipping Act to be registered.

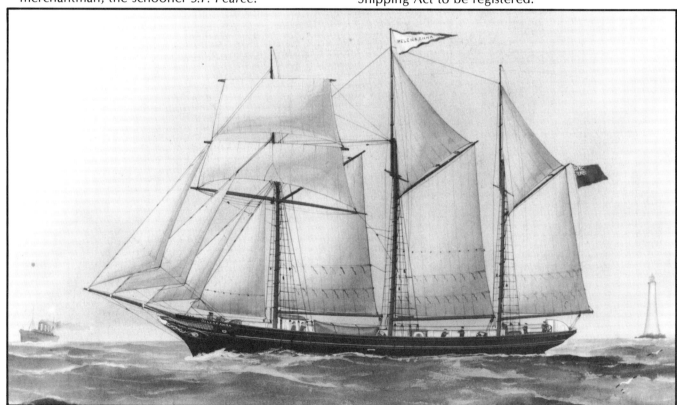

73 Registered at Fowey in 1892, owned by William Varcoe Kellow of Pentewan, the *Helena Anna* was built at Pekela, Holland in 1870. Laid up at Pont between the wars, she was requisitioned for use as a blockship in July 1940 at the entrance to Fowey harbour, foundering there six months later. Kellow also managed *Maria*, *Sarah Lightfoot*, *Traveller*, *Sterling*, *Volunteer* and *Tullochgorum*.

The official list as at the end of 1935 had 5 steamers (4 tugs, 1 yacht), of which one tug, the *Treffry*, had in fact ended her days the previous year stranded off Dunkirk. There were no cargo carrying steamers, the only one of that year having been transferred to Irvine, Scotland, in the November. This had been the 480-ton steel ss *Dunleary* bought in March 1933 by the Holden Steamship Company (H.E.B. Holden of Exmouth), and managed by the Fowey shipbroker Sydney James Samuel.

Where, on December 31 1920, there had been 39 Fowey ships, fifteen years later there were 54, but the difference — and more — had been brought about by the large number of new yachts, mostly of under 15 tons gross. And the port's shipping tonnage, down to 3,564 in 1920, was now a negligible 2,905.

BIGGEST CLAY PORT

By 1935, whether they were by sea or land, shipments out of what had become the world's biggest clay port were now all but totally by means that were owned elsewhere.

Although the small motor coaster had favoured Par and Charlestown, Fowey's rail-served deep water harbour enabled it to account for three or four times their tonnage. By 1935 the post-war plans to up-date it had matured. Where in 1920 one ship of 14,000 tons deadweight came in drawing 28 feet 3 inches of water and laid there for three months, the harbour could

now take vessels of up to 30 feet draught, on the tide. The main channel had a depth of 20 feet lwst to all jetties, of which there were now eight, three of them with electrical belt conveyors capable of 240 tons an hour. Yet, before it was taken up, this new big-ship capacity had to wait until well after 1945.

If they were lucky the port's shipwrights were employed on repair work or building pleasure or fishing craft. Anyone needing a new fishing boat or a yacht had a choice of first-class craftsmen. For yachts and boats at Fowey there were Percy Clemens and Archie Henry Watty. At Mevagissey, there was W. Frazier; at Portmellon, Percy G. Mitchell; and, at Looe, Frank Curtis, Peter Ferris and Arthur Collins. Especially in the 1930s Curtis built larger craft than others — a 46-ton motor yacht called *Anna Jane* in 1933, a motor schooner yacht *Anna Mena* of 30 tons in 1935 and various others.

The largest yacht by Slade's of Polruan had been a 14-ton yawl called *Foam* back in 1888. Their *Majub* for Captain Collins in 1928 was a 10-ton motor cutter and for Daphne du Maurier in 1929 there was the *Marie-Louise*, motor yawl.

After 1922 Slade's did little work. After they had completed the *A.B. Sherman* the bank that had backed them put in a receiver who remained till the war and then, inexplicably, the yard was idle throughout. Slade's neighbours at Polruan, C. Toms & Son, did not

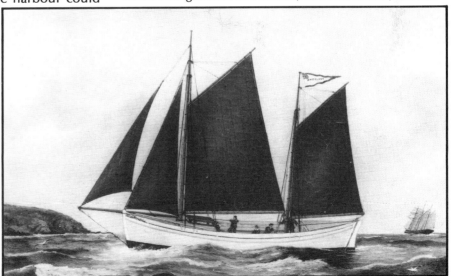

74 In Par Bay the ketch *White Lady*, 1906, with her owner aboard, Ben Tregaskes, the Par shipbuilder, and four of his seven sons. She was a redundant lifeboat 'from down Lizard way', re-built and re-rigged in the yard and liked so much that she was kept for personal use.

75 Shipyard high jinks, June 1918: shipwrights and apprentices from Heller's yard, Fowey, after hunting a whale that entered the harbour. Joined by a neighbouring young blacksmith who made the harpoon, they took French leave, commandeered one of Heller's boats and, after almost capsizing, killed and grounded their quarry. The carcass was returned to Neptune's care after yielding much needed supplies of bait.

begin building marine craft of any kind till the 1939 war when the Admiralty called upon them to do so, and they have continued ever since. The only other one-time builder of cargo vessels on the east bank of the Fowey, Butson's, had closed down about 1910.

HELLER'S

In Fowey town itself, a yard with a continuity that reached back to the days of the smuggling cutters was Heller's on Caffa Mill Pill. As I have said previously, William Brokenshaw built ships there from 1813 till his death in 1857. His yard was then carried on by a young partner who had been apprenticed to him in about

1844 — Richard Heller (1829—1904), sometimes 'Hellar'. After a spell at sea in the *Ant*, a Bristol vessel, Heller had been shipwrecked on the Magdalen Islands, Newfoundland and on returning home found employment for a time at Devonport Dockyard.

In 1882 Heller took a 99-year lease from the Treffry Estate of the yard at Caffa Mill Pill that became, for over thirty years, identified with his family name and where so many latter-day Fowey vessels were caulked, tarred, rigged and repaired. After his death his sons Richard William and William Henry carried on the business. The only vessel I am able to name that Heller built was the little ketch *Rival* of 1889, the last merchant sailing ship to be built in the port. The yard was taken over by the Fowey Coaling & Ship Repairing Company, which went into liquidation in 1924.

TREGASKES

However, the Tregaskes yard at Par went on working until 1957, with a record of all but a century behind it. As already stated, it had been started by Richard Tregaskes, shipwright, for Samuel Moss its owner, in the 1860s at the East Pier. Moss described himself as a Par shipbuilder at that period, subsequently as a Par or St. Austell merchant. He was not a shipwright but it was he who signed the builder's certificates as the master responsible, and he was the managing owner of a number of the vessels built in the yard. In the same records Richard Tregaskes is described as 'Polmear shipbuilder' in 1877 but not earlier.

Richard's son, Benjamin Moss Tregaskes, was apprenticed at the yard and served for a short time at sea, as was usual for many a shipwright. He worked for a spell in America, and on returning home about 1885 carried on the business. Then in 1893 he began building at Par, the only dry dock between Plymouth and Falmouth. This attracted a great deal of ship repair work and continued until the family firm, managed by his sons, ceased trading in 1957.

The yard built ten schooners and barquentines, registered at Fowey, of from 57—256 tons gross between 1867 and 1879. Additional to the seven named in a family memorandum headed 'Shipyard at Par', there were, I believe, three other schooners — the *Elizabeth Moss* of 1869, the *Dorothy* of 1871 and the *Mary Ann* of 1875. From 1880 the firm was occupied solely with repairs, boat building and war work.

GOODBYE 'WATERWITCH' AND 'JANE BANKS'

Par was the home of those two stalwarts, the *Waterwitch* and the *Jane Banks* which in 1936 were at last pressed into the great navy of unemployed. Their last masters respectively were Captains B.R. Carrick and G. Rundle. The *Waterwitch* had completed her last trip on May 7 1935, unloading her coal from Runcorn at Par — the last voyage by a British square rigger with cargo to a home port. The *Jane Banks* finished her days under the Red Ensign as the last Fowey merchant schooner to trade foreign. She had completed a Government charter, to Bermuda and Jamaica with coal, then with Government stores to and from the West Indies, thence home with wrecked stores. For this charter she was copper-bottomed anew but was lucky to complete the run home, leaking dangerously all the way, the last ninety miles without a rudder.

76 The dry dock at Par in 1952, built from 1893 by Benjamin Moss Tregaskes, of its kind unique in the West Country. Vessels rebuilt or repaired here included: *Adelaide, Alert, Bessie Stephens, Crystal Stream, Challenger, Dashing Wave, Devonia, Elizabeth Hill, Emeline Jenkin, Florence, Hannah, Helena Anna, Isabella, I'll Away, John Clark, John Farley, Jane Banks, Lizzie Trenberth, Little Pet, Little Gem, Little Mystery, Lydia Cardell, Maria, Mary Miller, Pedestrian, Perseverance, RTK, Rippling Wave, Sarah Lightfoot, Tullochgorum, Traveller* and *Waterwitch*. From other ports, home and abroad, came many others.
National Maritime Museum

77 *Jane Banks* (a) port deck (b) starboard deck.

On February 22 1938 the *Jane Banks* was sold by the Stephens family for £235 to an Estonian and after refit left Par for the last time on April 29 under the saddened gaze of, among many others, Captain Bob May whose father had bought her as the *Frau Minna Petersen* nearly forty years previously. They did say that her copper alone could have fetched the price paid for her. She traded under another name in the Baltic for six more years and was then lost in a gale off the coast of Finland.

At an asking price of £325, the *Waterwitch* also went to the Estonians a year after the *Jane Banks*, having been cleaned up and repaired by Tregaskes to get her to Board of Trade standard to sail away. Reaching her new home in the Gulf of Finland in thirty days from Par (Greenhill says in *The Merchant Schooners*) she made £200 in her first five months carrying timber.

ONE LAST BRAVE ESSAY

Yet amid all this change and decay one last brave essay in local ship ownership was to be attempted and with the most up-to-date vessels. Where in the 1890s Toyne Carter had gone into steam management with their six 350—500 ton ships, a venture terminated by post-war depression, so now did Hannan, Samuel & Company, Fowey's other leading shipbrokers, try their hand with motor cargo ships.

78 *Jane Banks* leaving Par for the last time, spring 1938.
Mr. J.H. Samuel

This firm had been founded by William Francis Hannan, who had married Kate, the daughter of John Henry Hocken, to whose family of mariners and shipowners I have already referred. Hannan in 1884

became managing owner of their brigantines *Concord*, *Wild Wave* and *Maria Luigia* and, at about the same time, set up as shipbroker, also going into ownership on his own account (the brigantine *Perseverance* in 1888).

On Hannan's death in about 1900 the business was carried on by his younger son, John Henry Hannan, (d. 1913), first partnered by E.H. Bennett, then by Sydney James Samuel (d. 1949), his brother-in-law. In 1920 S.J. Samuel, the surviving partner, was joined by K.G. Spratt, who was succeeded in 1946 by John Hocken Samuel, S.J.'s son and great-grandson of John Henry Hocken whose great-great-grandson indeed, Anthony, runs the business to this day.

The venture into motor cargo vessels was made jointly by S.J. Samuel and Stafford Frank Hough, O.B.E., then manager of Coast Lines of Falmouth, originally known as Powell, Hough & Bacon of Liverpool, and grandson of one of its founders. In the 1930s the two men worked together on the idea of a Cornish shipping company

80 With his wife, John Henry Hannan (d. 1913) who continued the Fowey shipbroking business after his father's death in about 1900.
Mr. J.H. Samuel

79 About 1900: Sydney James Samuel, the Fowey shipbroker, who was brother-in-law and partner of William Francis Hannan, the son-in-law of John Henry Hocken (d. 1892), master mariner, ship chandler, bank agent and shipowner.
Mr. J.H. Samuel

that, among other things, would carry china clay mainly to the Baltic and bring back timber to the West Country. For this purpose they formed the H & S Shipping Company Ltd. (changed to Polpen Shipping Company in 1939), encouraged by a number of well-known Cornish families who became shareholders. S.J. Samuel was manager.

Late in 1937 the new firm took delivery of a motor cargo vessel, the *Polperro*, specially built under contract for it by Muller & Broerken, of Foxhol, Groningen, Holland. She carried 530 tons, measured 145 x 26 x 9 feet, was built of steel, joggled, with cruiser stern and modern raked soft bows. A year later, a sister ship, the *Poldhu*, with only minor improvements, was also brought into commission. Both were fitted with new 360 bhp 6 cyl Brons diesels, giving a service speed of 10½ knots.

81 A good view of the hull of the *Polperro* in the builder's yard — Muller & Broerken, Foxhol, Groningen.

Mr. J.H. Samuel

A third ship was in fact contracted for, to carry 750 tons. She was completed at Foxhol but owing to the outbreak of war could not be delivered, Holland then being neutral. She was sold to Swedish Lloyd in Stockholm and became *Sigbritt*. Indeed, a fourth ship had also been ordered, from a British builder, but while she was still on the stocks the contract was taken over by the Minister of War Transport.

These acquisitions were calculated to put Fowey ship management into a completely new, forward-looking phase. Alas, everything was right except, as it turned out, the luck.

Sixteen months after the *Poldhu* went to work she was wrecked at Ile de Sein, Pointe du Raz, Finistere, a total loss. Her recovery had to wait till after the war when, in 1946, a certificate of seaworthiness enabled her to be re-registered. Seven years later she was transferred to London and, after several changes of ownership, re-named *Roselyn*. She was still afloat up to a couple of years ago though under the Greek flag and yet another name.

The *Polperro* was even less fortunate. In the winter of 1943/44 she was sunk by enemy action.

END OF AN ERA

On the outbreak of war in September 1939 only six of the 58 vessels on the register were cargo carriers. In addition to the *Polperro* and *Poldhu* there were the three schooners *S.F. Pearce*, German built in 1908; the *Mary Miller*, built in 1881 and the Dutch-built *Helena Anna*, at sixty-nine years the oldest vessel on the register; also the auxiliary ketch of 1897, the *Isabel*.

In 1940 the *Helena Anna* was commandeered and sunk as a blockship at the entrance to Fowey harbour. The *Mary Miller* had the distinction of being, by 1939, one of the only three engineless schooners under the Red Ensign, the others being the Irish-owned *Brooklands* (formerly *Susan Vittery*) and the *Katie* of Padstow. She was laid up, sold for a yacht after the war and finished her days somewhere as a house-boat. The steel *S.F. Pearce* was sold in 1941 to William Cooper & Son of Widnes, turned into a towing barge on the Mersey, and broken up in 1960. The little *Isabel* survived the war to have new engines installed in her in 1947, 1950 and 1974, a yacht eventually lost off the coast of Brazil.

The only other Fowey working vessels were 10 harbour craft: the tugs *Gallant*, *Penleath* and *Pendennick*; 4

82 *Katie* of Padstow under economy canvas. She was owned jointly and personally from 1931 by partners in Clunes & Company, Par coal factors and builders' merchants. One of them, Edward Stephens, managed her but his joint interest lapsed with him when he died in 1935. By 1947 she had passed to a marine engineer who sold her to Danish owners. She was re-named *Bergfalk*, and ended her days as a house-boat.

83 Master and crew probably of the *Bessie Stephens* in 1917. Captain Deacon had transferred to her after the sinking of the *Ocean Swell* by enemy action only to have his new command sent to the bottom by submarine a few months later. He is standing second from left.

Mrs. Goldie Facey, Charlestown

barges and 3 dredgers. The rest of the port's ships were yachts — 42 of them averaging 13 tons, the largest the 46-ton *Anna Jane*, Looe-built in 1933 and Lancashire-owned. Five yachts were taken over by the Government for one purpose or another: *Twinkle*, *Little Gypsy*, *Meander*, *Galahad II* and *Adeline*.

PORTRAIT OF A COASTING SEAMAN

Nearing the end of this narrative, I am conscious of having given too little attention to various aspects of it, not least the masters and crews who risked not merely cash but life and limb manning the little ships that are its subject. So, hoping that it might remedy the

84 Captain Charles Henry Deacon (1862—1935) of Charlestown — an oil portrait by Arthur Bradbury ARWS who served under him in the *Waterwitch*.

94

omission in some way I have chosen for special treatment one of their company to represent them — Charles Henry Deacon (1862—1935), a man typical of the best of British coasting masters and, in character, belonging to the same tradition as that other coasting seaman of 150 years earlier, Captain James Cook, R.N.

Like many of his calling, he was a conservative traditionalist, fifty-five years in sailing vessels, forty of them in the service of one family of owners. He was deeply religious, a teetotaller, non-smoker and non-swearer. Yet he always commanded respect and often deep affection from his crews, colleagues and superiors.

He was born in Beesands on Start Bay, Devon, a fishing hamlet almost destroyed on various occasions by inundation from the seas breaking across the treacherous banks of rock and gravel due east of it called the Skerries.

At first he worked on a farm but, at eighteen, he went to sea in a Cardiff schooner, the *Ezel*. Voyaging took him to Charlestown where, in 1885, he married a local girl and made his home.

In 1890, at twenty-seven years of age he was given his first command, by Richard Harris Williams, a St. Austell mining engineer, of the 116-ton schooner *Fortunate* of Fowey, built at Padstow 1874. As well as this and a similar schooner called the *Frances*, Williams owned the Mevagissey built *Brenton*, and when he sold her in 1894 to John Stephens of Par, Deacon went over to Stephens as her master. Four years later when the schooner *St. Germans* (later *Little Belle*) was bought, he briefly took her over, and then another acquisition, the 199-ton Prince Edward Islander brigantine *Fortune*, after which he stayed in square riggers for the rest of his life, with only one brief exception.

Like many another coasting master, Deacon had no formal qualification but when Edward Stephens early in 1899 bought the barquentine *Ocean Swell* which his father had built at Fowey twenty-four years previously, Deacon was not only thoroughly experienced, he enjoyed the warm friendship and complete confidence of the family that employed him. So from the time they bought her he had command of the *Ocean Swell*, the fleet's flagship. Yet he only once held shares in Stephens's ships — 5/64ths in the *Brenton* which he lost when she was wrecked at Smoky Tickle, Labrador, in 1900.

85 Built by William Walters at Bideford 1859, the *St. Germans* was bought forty years later by John Stephens, transferred from Plymouth to Fowey and re-named *Little Belle*. She is pictured here off the Eddystone, in an oil painting, done for Captain Simon Tabb, her master, by Reuben Chappell c. 1904.

Mr. N. Purdie, Holmbush, St. Austell

Meanwhile, Mrs. Deacon's sister had met and married a 21-year old Welsh seaman named George Beynon who, probably introduced by his brother-in-law, joined Stephens in 1897/98, became mate of the *Ocean Swell*, then master of the *Fortune* in 1901 and others of the fleet. The two men became close friends. Beynon was seven or eight years younger than Deacon, a big man with a reputation for hard driving yet liked by his men. Both men were confirmed square riggers, and neither would have any truck with 'steamboats'.

Deacon would never put to sea on a Sunday when, in the afternoon, he read the Bible that was always with him. Some of his methods might have come down from the Elizabethans. To gauge his ship's speed in light airs he would drop wood shavings or bits of paper over the bow, then time them to the stern. At one time he was bearded but, in the 1914—18 war, ashore on the French coast, he was misunderstood and, instead of trimming it, the *barbier* took half of it off before he could be stopped, so the other half had to go too. At times he wore a sealskin cap of a kind usually badly cured, believed by some to cause baldness. Also characteristic were his gold earrings and leather thigh boots. Usually, too, he wore a Guernsey that was hand-knitted in the old way with, on either shoulder, a rib for each of his children.

He commanded the *Ocean Swell* for eighteen years until she was sunk by enemy submarine on July 5 1917 in the English Channel. After that, for six months, he had the 110-ton *Bessie Stephens*, a schooner built at Par in 1878, his only departure from square rigs in thirty-five years. On February 14 1918 she too was lost by submarine — within twenty miles of the latitude and longtitude that he claimed had been foretold to him in a dream as to where she would be sunk. On July 6 he took over the ship with which from then on his name was always coupled: the barquentine *Waterwitch*, which Stephens had only recently acquired and now had partly rebuilt.

Mainly carrying china clay and coal cargoes, the *Waterwitch* at that time was one of the very few British square riggers trading out of the UK and, before she was sold foreign in 1938, was to become the last under the Red Ensign from a home port.

Under Deacon she became one of the best-known ships in the merchant service. Until 1937, to qualify as Trinity House pilots candidates had to serve for twelve months in a square rigged vessel, so a stream of young men, many with master's certificates, served under Deacon, signed on as mates but working as crew. This and his remarkable seamanship made both ship and master into something like celebrities. No doubt, too, his characterful 'newsworthiness' had something to do with it — he was a gift to reporters despite his quiet-spoken modesty.

Meanwhile his brother-in-law, George Beynon, had been appointed in 1920 to the command of Stephens's other barquentine, the *Lydia Cardell*, now retired to coasting after 40 years of trading across the Western Ocean and down to the Mediterranean. He had her for nine years until she was run down by a steamer.

Now turned seventy, in 1934 the old master of the *Waterwitch* retired, but never recovered from the shock of his brother-in-law's death the previous year. Married to sisters, each had had eight children. Both families lived in Charlestown, and both men had been friends and colleagues for over forty years. Each was a square rig skipper — each had had two ships shot from under him.

'Charlie' Deacon died in May 1935, quietly proud that in forty-five years' command of coasting vessels he had lost none by accident.

A CENTURY-AND-A-HALF OF CHANGE

The changes that occurred in the port's ships over the 150 years that ended in 1939 were probably greater than in any previous period of similar duration.

In 1786 the craft best suited to local needs was probably a wooden, wind-propelled sloop that could take sixty or seventy tons of cargo. By 1939 it had to be a diesel-fuelled, steel-hulled vessel with much the same crew but capable of carrying at least ten times that weight. In the jargon of economics, assets that were once labour intensive were now capital intensive. In 1850 the 138 merchant ships that belonged to the port employed 700 seamen. Within a hundred years the equivalent figures had declined to proportions too negligible to warrant quotation.

The fact is that vessels owned, registered and manned elsewhere increasingly carried the port's trade more efficiently and economically than could be sustained locally, perhaps because there were other investment opportunities considered to be better paying than ships, china clay itself for example.

It is true that with good management, sailing vessels large and small, ocean-going and coasting, might make enough cash in their first ten years to pay for their capital cost — *Ocean Ranger* and *E.S. Hocken* certainly did, and there were no doubt others whose accounts we do not have. And in days when 3% Consols were the giltest of gilt-edged securities, 10% per annum from a high risk business was a good return. But I doubt whether the ships of Fowey earned that generally. Probably more characteristic was the profitability of the *Maggie C.* of 1877. She took ten years to earn 58% of her 'first cost'. Had she survived after 1887 higher repair and maintenance demands must have lessened the likelihood of continuance of that order of return.

The collapse of local investment in shipping, as reflected in the number of merchantmen registered in the port, was presaged by the ending of local wooden ship-building in the 1870s. And that in turn had its origin in the early use of iron instead of wood not only for leviathans like the *Great Britain* (1843) and the *Great Eastern* (1854) but for vessels of much the same size and form as were typical of Fowey at the time. The first iron-hulled vessel launched on the Wear at Sunderland — England's biggest shipbuilding centre — was a schooner, the *Loftus* of 1852, 77 tons. Iron — and of course its successor, steel — made incomparably larger ships possible; and the coast between Plymouth and Falmouth apart from anything else, was not suited to big ship-building.

For big ships the essentials were sheltered, deep water (which was available at Fowey) and plenty of shore space (which was not). Such were limitations of one kind or another that the *Jane Slade* and some other vessels had to be launched sideways, and at Bodinnick care had to be taken that a vessel launched end on did not go ashore on the opposite bank.

Gales were a danger to hulls on the stocks, and it was the normal aim to complete a vessel by September and get her into the water for rigging. Providing it was no later than March, the date she was laid down mattered less as, in the early stages, she presented little resistance to wind. Butson started the schooner *Gallant* in October 1838 and the shipwrights and joiners finished on September 3 1839. But a hull could be built in much less than eleven months, and six months was not uncommon. It is significant that where, in the 18th century, cargo ships were built on the beach and other sites between the Dodman and Looe — even pinched-in Polperro is recorded as a place of origin of a few, though the actual birth-place was probably nearby Talland Bay — by 1880 they had dwindled to one only, the one where the port's largest vessels were built, in the north-facing protective crescent of Polruan; notably, and more specifically, in the most westerly yard below its West Street. The village gets half its name from its pool, probably better sheltered from the strongest gales than anywhere along this coast, yet with deep water and just enough shore room to accommodate the laying down of vessels of up to about 400 tons.

The few craft built in the 1960s on Polruan's Brazen Island were of the order of 340—370 tons. The 623-ton *A.B. Sherman* had to be re-built in the mud of Pont Pill, where Slade's prepared the ground for a patent slipway, although it never arrived and, anyway, the 1920 slump completely nullified the project.

BIG-SHIP EXPERIENCE

As labour costs, mechanisation and better land transport caused small cargoes to become less and less worth handling, small vessels that were once useful became obsolete, not worth replacing. Also, despite its capacity for ships of substantial tonnage, whatever the cause Fowey seems always to have been the home of vessels essentially small. Most owners of the few Fowey ships that were larger than 300 tons either disposed of them as soon as they could get an acceptable price, or were unlucky with them, or both. Of ships of this size, ignoring a few harbour craft, there were only ever sixteen.

Of these it must first be said that three, all Canadian softwood barques, were managed successfully at Fowey for twenty-five, thirteen and sixteen years respectively — the *Royal Adelaide* (410 tons), the *Good Intent* (593) and the *George Arkle* (553). Also, later on, four of Toyne Carter's fleet of six steamers ran under local colours, so to speak, for from seventeen to twenty-five years, although despite this, at Fowey steam hardly survived the first World War's aftermath.

Of our sixteen, nine were sold (three of them within three years of acquisition) and seven were lost. Of the latter the biggest, the 761-ton barque *Bangalore* of 1857 was abandoned at sea in November of that year. The Sunderland-built square rigger *Platina* (303 tons) of 1863 was lost within three years on voyage to Quebec. The former American brigantine *Beatrice Rillston* (399) was stranded on the coast of Cyprus five months after being bought. The ss *Norma* of 1899 had to be abandoned in a sinking condition after three years. The motor ship *Polperro* of 1938 was sunk by enemy action in 1944 and her sister the *Poldhu* was wrecked a year after purchase.

To these sixteen Fowey ships one might add the *Rigdin* (397 tons) but she was never transferred from the Southampton register, being found to have much too much draught for the purpose for which she was

86 The motor cargo vessel *Polperro* of 1938, 403 tons, sunk by enemy action 1944. She had a sister ship, the *Poldhu* of 1939. Both were built in Holland for the H.& S. Shipping Co. of Fowey. War prevented delivery of two similar vessels that were on order. The *Poldhu* was wrecked in 1940, re-registered post-war, transferred to London 1953. Frustrated by war, these were Fowey's one and only venture into motor ships.

Mr. J.H. Samuel

bought. Neither can one say that local experience with the New England built *A.B. Sherman*, sold in 1923, was anything but calamitous, though no worse than many another ship worldwide at that time.

No common denominator other than size seems to apply to this apparent pattern.

It also seems remarkable that, with an exporting industry at its back so substantial and vigorous as china clay, local investment in ships shrank to vanishing point. One reason may be that, while clay cargoes were usually there for the asking, relative to others they gave the shipowner a very low return, if any.

In the days of sail some clay merchants reckoned it paid them to take shares in vessels that carried their products, and in modern times the unreliable condition of many ships led the industry into shipowning in a very limited way. Aside from anything else, dirty holds and faulty hatch covers can contaminate clay cargoes with disastrous consequences. But even a limited 'do-it-yourself' policy by clay shippers became less and less worthwhile as standards were improved.

Of recent years, while the industry has understandably sought to control all operations affecting it, ensuring this through ownership has stopped short at shipside. The clay shippers found they were best off when they left it wholly to others to compete for the business of carrying their products oversea. While it is in the interest of the shipowner to optimise freights, the very opposite is true of the shipper. And ship-owning by shippers might compromise that balance. Ships and ship management, too, have a distinct expertise that has become more and more complex.

87 The Cowes-built cutter yacht *Betty*, hulked at Par, 1938. Bought for her spars, lead, sails and gear 1918 and then cannibalised — a macabre end in her 21st year for a Royal Yacht Squadron aristocrat.

SOURCES

Treasury Warrant, Trinity Term, 29 Charles II and Court of Exchequer Return February 17 1841 (Limits of Port & Legal Quays).

Acts of Parliament: 26 George III, cap. 60 (Ship Registration)
24 George III, cap. 47
27 George III, cap. 32 — (Customs laws and rules filled 'six large folio volumes unprovided with any index'. In 1810 digest of them occupied 1,375 pages. — Graham Smith below).

H.M. Customs Registers of British Shipping at the Port of Fowey 1786—1890 at County Record Office, Truro, and later years at Custom House, Fowey.

H.M. Custom House Sea Fishing Boat Registers. Records of the Registrar General of Shipping & Seamen (BT162 & BT163), PRO, Kew, London.

Census of Population 1801

Lloyd's Register of Shipping

County Record Office, Truro: Half-yearly Agreements and accounts of Voyages and Crews (MSR488); the Treffry Papers (TF826).

Fowey Harbour Commissioners, minutes from 1869.

National Maritime Museum collections of documents: Toyne, Carter & Company; Stephens; Tregaskes.

China Clay Working Party Report (HMSO 1948).

Account book of the *Maggie C* (Fowey Town Museum).

Account books of: *Fancy, Sally, Mary Ann & Eliza, Rachel Anne;* also freight book of *Trewartha* (author's possession).

Account books of Hocken family: Ship chandlery: Sails; Copper & Yellow Metal; *Ocean Ranger, Ocean Spray, E.S. Hocken* (Mr. J.H. Samuel, Feock, Cornwall).

Guide to the St. Austell China Clay Museum 1975.

Steele's List of the Royal Navy 1814.

Cornish Guardian: Cornish heritage series October 10 1957 to February 1 1962; Richard Heller obituary December 16 1904; End of shipbuilding at Par April 4 1957; Brazen Island Shipyard July 7 1960.

West Briton: Sale of Geach property at Polruan June 19 1840.

Abell, Sir Westcott	*The Shipwright's Trade* (Cambridge University Press, 1948)
Ackland, N.A. & Druce, R.M.	*Lanteglos by Fowey: The Story of a Parish* (Fowey 1978)
Atton, H. & Holland, H.H.	*The King's Customs* (London 1918)
Bainbridge,. George	*The Wooden Ships & the Iron Men of the Cornish China Clay Trade* (Charlestown 1980)
Barton, D.B.	*A Historical Survey of the Mines & Mineral Railways of East Cornwall & West Devon* (D. Bradford Barton, Truro 1971)
Barton, R.M.	*A History of the Cornish China Clay Industry* (D. Bradford Barton, Truro 1966)
	Life in Cornwall in the 19th Century 4 vols. (extracts from the *West Briton*) (D. Bradford Barton, Truro 1970—1974)
Bradbury, Arthur	'Aboard the Barquentine *Waterwitch*' article in *Ships & Ship Models*, May 1932
Clements, Paul	*Marc Isembard Brunel* (London 1970)
Coysh, Victor	*The Guernsey Shipbuilding Industry* (Transactions of La Société Guernesiaise XV 1952)
Couch, Jonathan	*The History of Polperro*, 1871 (Frank Graham, Newcastle-upon-Tyne 1965)
Dewar-Brown, W.	'The Little Ships of Troy' series of nine articles, *The Cornish Magazine*, March—November 1962, Falmouth
Duncan, Jonathan	*The History of Guernsey* (London 1841)
Dyson, John	*Business in Great Waters* (London 1977)
Falconer, William	*Marine Dictionary* (London 1815)
Farr, Grahame	'Custom House Ship Registers', article in *The Mariner's Mirror*, February 1969
	'Custom House Ship Registers of the West Country', paper in *The South-west & The Sea* ed. H.E.S. Fisher (University of Exeter 1968)
Gill, Crispin	*Plymouth, A New History* Vol 2. (David & Charles 1979)
Greenhill, Basil	*The Merchant Schooners* 2 vols. 1951 (National Maritime Museum 1978)
	Schooners (B.T. Batsford 1980)
	The Ship 1815–1965 (HMSO 1980)
	'My Girl Friend Ingrid' in Maritime monograph No. 36 (National Maritime Museum, 1978)
Greenhill, Basil & Giffard, Ann	*Westcountrymen in Prince Edward's Isle* (Toronto University Press 1974)
Hadfield, Charles	*The Canals of South-west England* (David & Charles 1967)
Hobbs, J.S.	*The British Channel Pilot* (London 1859)
Hudson, Kenneth	*The History of English China Clays* (David & Charles c. 1970)
Isham, Kenneth	'The Day of the Lime Kiln', article in *Western Morning News*, December 16 1966
Jarvis, Rupert C.	'Sources for the History of Ports' article in *Journal of Transport History III* (1957—1958)
Jenkin, A.K. Hamilton	*Cornwall & its People* (J.M. Dent & Sons 1945)
Kemp, Peter (Ed.)	*The Oxford Companion to Ships and the Sea* (Oxford University Press 1976)

King, John W. — *The Pilot's Handbook for the English Channel* (London 1869)

Halliday, F.E. — *A History of Cornwall* (Gerald Duckworth 1959)

Knight, Frank — *A Beginner's Guide to the Sea* (Macmillan & Co. 1956)

Leland, John — 'Itinerary' in *Early Tours in Devon & Cornwall*, ed. R. Pearse Chope (David & Charles 1967)

Lloyd, Edward — *Encyclopaedic Dictionary* 7 vols. (London 1895)

Lubbock, Basil — *The Last of the Windjammers* 2 vols. (Brown, Son & Ferguson, Glasgow 1929)

Mogg, Edward — *Paterson's Roads* (London 1829)

Munn, Robert S. — *British Coasters & Newfoundland Traders* two articles in *Sea Breezes*, May & June 1933

Pearse, Richard — *The Ports & Harbours of Cornwall* (H.E. Warne, St. Austell 1963)

Rashleigh, E.W. — *A Short History of the Town & Borough of Fowey* 1887 (Fowey Old Cornwall Society 1964)

Richards, John — 'Bygone Polruan' article in *Old Cornwall*, Vol. VIII No. 9 (Federation of Old Cornwall Societies)

Rowe, John — *Cornwall in the Age of the Industrial Revolution* (Liverpool 1953)

Rowse, A.L. — *Tudor Cornwall* (Jonathan Cape 1941, 1943)

Shore, Henry N. (Lord Teignmouth) — *Smuggling Days & Smuggling Ways* (Cassell 1892)

Old Foye Days Vol. 1 (Clevedon Printing Co. 1896)

Shore, Henry N. (Lord Teignmouth) — *Old Foye Days* Vol. 2 'The Smugglers of Fowey' 1907 (Frank Graham, Newcastle-upon-Tyne 1966)

The Smugglers 2 Vols. (with Charles G. Harper) (Cecil Palmer 1923)

Smith, Graham — *Something to Declare* (Harrap 1980)

Smith, J.W. & Holden, T.S. — *Where Ships are Born* (Sunderland 1953)

Spreadbury, I.D. ('Kerdroya') — *Fowey – A Brief History* (Fowey Old Cornwall Society 4th ed. c. 1981)

Tupper, F.B. — *The History of Guernsey & its Bailiwick* (2nd ed. London 1876)

Varcoe, Jonathan — 'Cornish Boat Ownership in the 1870s', article in *Western Morning News*, April 12 1979

'The *Treffry* of Par', article in *Sea Breezes*, November 1977

Varcoe, Phillip — *China Clay: The Early Years* (Francis Antony, St. Austell 1978)

Ward-Jackson, C.H. — 'The Ships of the Port of Fowey at the Turn of the 18th Century', paper in *Ports & Shipping in the South-west*, ed. H.E.S. Fisher (University of Exeter 1971)

Last Log of the Schooner 'Isabella', Maritime monograph No. 24 (National Maritime Museum 1976)

Stephens of Fowey, Maritime monograph No. 43 (National Maritime Museum 1980)

White, Margaret — *The Carteret Priaulx Papers: The Influence of the Napoleonic Wars on Guernsey.* (Transactions of La Société Guernesiaise XVII 1963)

APPENDIX 'A'

NUMBER OF SHIPS ON THE FOWEY REGISTER AS AT DECEMBER 31

As returned to the Registrar General of Shipping (PRO BT162 & BT163).   Averages to nearest ton.

1792   52 ships averaging 46 tons (employing 214 men/boys).

1850   137 ships averaging 78 tons (employing 685 men/boys).

1905   101 ships averaging 124 tons (91 sail averaging 112 tons; 10 steam averaging 23 tons).

1910   79 ships averaging 119 tons (68 sail averaging 110 tons; 11 steam averaging 209 tons).

1935   54 ships averaging 54 tons (15 'sail' averaging 123 tons but including 7 dredgers, barges, *etc*; 5 steam averaging 71 tons; 34 motor averaging 21 tons).

1950   76 ships averaging 37 tons (9 'sail' averaging 84 tons but including 4 dredgers, barges, *etc*; 4 steam averaging 103 tons; 63 motor averaging 26 tons).

APPENDIX 'B'

KINDS & SIZES OF SHIPS REGISTERED

KIND OF SHIP	1786—1815		1816—1840		1841—1880		1881—1920		1921—1939	
	No.	Av. tons	No.	Av. tons	No.	Av. tons	No.	Av. tons	No.	Av. tons
Barges & lighters	37	57	5	42	—	—	—	—	6	166
Dredgers	—	—	—	—	—	—	—	—	2	84
Barquentines	—	—	—	—	4	274	6	200	—	—
Barques	1	239	—	—	*10	399	1	262	—	—
Boats	6	17	—	—	—	—	—	—	—	—
Brigs	6	122	2	136	7	184	2	182	—	—
Brigantines	47		7	116	53	149	18	206	—	—
Galliasses	1	153	—	—	—	—	—	—	—	—
Ketches	1	66	—	—	2	34	11	38	—	—
Launches, motor	—	—	—	—	—	—	—	—	3	5
Luggers	27	77	—	—	5	18	2	8	—	—
Motor ships	—	—	—	—	—	—	—	—	5	285
Schooners	32	48	79	88	189	99	49	139	3	317
Shallops	3	50	1	19	—	—	—	—	—	—
Ships, full rigged	4	258	—	—	—	—	—	—	—	—
Sloops & cutters	273	57	76	46	**26	39	**15	20	—	—
Smacks	3	43	7	49	11	41	1	31	—	—
Steamers***	—	—	—	—	3	69	14	211	4	285
Yachts, sail or motor	—	—	—	—	—	—	1	3	32	22
Yawls	—	—	1	13	9	30	9	14	—	—
	441	68	178	67	319	110	129	98	55	93

*including one of 198 tons described as a 'Barquette'.
**probably including some yachts.   ***including steam yachts and tugs.

APPENDIX 'C'

FATE OF SHIPS REGISTERED AT FOWEY FROM 1786 TO 1939

	1786—1815	1816—1840	1841—1880	1881—1920	1921—1939
Transferred to Guernsey	59	2	—	—	—
Transferred to other ports	150	76	80	24	4
Lost by foundering, stranding, *etc.*	105	73	165	43	4
Abandoned at sea	—	2	10	7	—
Absent, missing	—	1	8	1	—
Lost by enemy action	—	—	6	6	3
Taken by the enemy	15	—	—	—	—
Seized for smuggling, condemned & 'broke', ripped up or sold	81	2	—	—	—
Broken up	6	12	27	13	9
Ripped up	7	1	—	—	—
Sold foreign	3	—	5	15	5
Acquired by Government (Navy Board, Ministry of Shipping, *etc.*	1	—	—	3	5
Hulked	1	1	14	4	—
Fate unrecorded	7	3	—	1	—
Register cancelled or closed for unrecorded reason	5	4	3	7	2
Registered *de novo* at unrecorded date	1	—	—	—	—
Register closed on conversion to barge or lighter	—	1	1	3	—
Still registered end 1939	—	—	—	2	23
Total	441	178	319	129	55

PORTS OF BUILD OF SHIPS* REGISTERED AT FOWEY
1786 TO 1939

Built in:	30 yrs. 1786—1815	25 yrs. 1816—1840	40 yrs. 1841—1880	40 yrs. 1881—1920	19 yrs. 1921—1939
Cornwall	70%	77%	45%	28%	51%
Fowey	68%	74%	33%	9%	42%
Devon	12%	15%	19%	18%	7%
Other English	5%	3%	·10%	20%	18%
Scotland	—	1%	5%	17%	7%
Wales	1%	1%	5%	6%	—
Ireland		1%	—	2%	2%
Channel Islands	1%	—	—	1%	—
Canada		2%	13%	2%	—
Foreign		—	3%	6%	11%
Prizes of War	11%	—	—	—	—
Unrecorded	—	—	—	—	4%
Number of ships	441	178	319	129**	55***
Average per annum	15	7	8	3	3

*Not including those entered on the Sea Fishing Boat Register introduced from 1902.
**Of which 22 were pleasure craft, 14 of them less than 15 tons.
***Of which 37 were pleasure craft, 25 of them less than 15 tons.
Percentages are to the nearest single figure.

APPENDIX 'E'

MERCHANT SHIPS OF KNOWN BUILDER, BUILT AND REGISTERED AT FOWEY
1786—1880***

The ships and tonnages below represent about 70% of the vessels built and registered in the port during the period (55% 1786—1815, 81% 1816—1840, 92% 1841—1880). Additionally, unknown numbers were built and registered initially elsewhere. These estimates are believed to provide a dependable indication of the *relative* size of outputs. All figures are rounded off.

1786—1815
30 years

	Mevagissey*	Charlestown	Par	Fowey	Polruan & Bodinnick	Looe**	Total
Tonnage	8,533	—	—	3,188	244	—	11,965
Tonnage per year	284	—	—	106	8	—	399
Number of ships	110	—	—	43	6	—	159
Average tonnage per ship	78	—	—	74	41	—	75

1816—1840
25 years

	Mevagissey*	Charlestown	Par	Fowey	Polruan & Bodinnick	Looe**	Total
Tonnage	2,005	680	—	3,065	2,166	—	7,916
Tonnage per year	80	27	—	123	87	—	317
Number of ships	25	10	—	39	33	—	107
Average tonnage per ship	80	68	—	79	68	—	74

1841—1880
40 years

	Mevagissey*	Charlestown	Par	Fowey	Polruan & Bodinnick	Looe**	Total
Tonnage	1,065	1,345	1,442	2,190	3,718	890	10,650
Tonnage per year	27	34	36	55	93	22	266
Number of ships	13	13	11	21	30	9	97
Average tonnage per ship	82	107	131	99	124	99	110

*Including Portmellon.

**Not included in Port of Fowey until 1841.

***After 1880 (with one minor exception in 1888) yachts and boats only were built until the 1950s when some vessels were built on Brazen Island, Polruan.

Tonnage by location 1786–1880

Mevagissey	11,603
Fowey	8,443
Looe	890
Charlestown	2,025
Polruan & Bodinnick	6,128
Par	1,442

PORT OF FOWEY BUILDERS' SHIPS REGISTERED 1786—1939
With year of registration and rig

ALLEN, John, at Mevagissey 1797—1800.
Vertumnus 1797 slp — Active 1799 ctr — Rose 1799 ctr — Pearl 1800 ctr.

ANGEAR, James, at East Looe 1903.
Sweet Home 1932 yht.

BANKS, William Pearse, at Charlestown 1816—1836.
Kitty & Clara 1816 slp — Harriot 1818 ctr — Union Packet 1823 slp — Charles Rashleigh 1824 sch — Henry 1824 sch — Gleaner 1827 slp — Laurel 1832 slp — East Cornwall 1834 sch — Busy 1836 slp.

BROKENSHAW, William, at Fowey 1813—1857.
Heed 1813 sch — George 1816 sch — Place 1819 slp — Emerald 1820 sch — Richard & Jane 1829 slp — Excellent 1832 sch — Charlotte & Maria 1833 sch — John Carnall 1833 sch — Honour 1834 sch — Lavinia 1835 slp — One & All 1836 slp — Richard Carnall 1837 sch — Standard 1837 slp — Touch-Me-Not 1841 sch — Need 1845 slp — Enterprise 1846 sch — Eliza Hanson 1852 sch — Ann Beer 1857 sch.

BUTSON, Nicholas, succeeded by Nicholas and Joseph, at Polruan and Bodinnick 1839—1875.
Gallant 1839 sch — Model 1840 slp — Sabina 1841 sch — Alert 1842 sch — John Wesley 1848 sch — Amelia 1849 lgr — William Morgan Davies 1857 sch — Thomas Aylan 1860 sch — Rebecca 1862 sch — Bessie 1863 sch — Rippling Wave 1869 sch — Gem 1871 bgn — Thetis 1873 sch — Undine 1875 bgn.

COLLINS, Arthur, at East Looe 1926.
Pendragon 1926 lnh.

CURTIS, Frank, at East Looe 1932—1937.
Shaheen 1932 yht — Little Gipsy 1932 yht — Gracian (Sea Maiden from 1935) 1932 yht — Ichneumon (Melody Maid from 1946) 1933 yht — White Fox II 1933 yht — Makera 1933 yht — Anna Jane 1933 yht — Smew 1934 yht — Anne Mena (Adeline from 1936) 1935 yht — Natsopa 1937 yht.

DINGLE, Albertus, at Fowey 1880.
Zingari (Little Pet from 1888) Plymouth 1880 Fowey 1888 sch.

DUNN, James, succeeded by Walter at Mevagissey and/or Portmellon 1800—1842.
Lord Nelson 1800 ctr — Mary 1802 lgr — Venus 1802 ctr — Hiram 1802 ctr — Ranger 1805 ctr — Jane 1806 ctr — Fame 1807 ctr — Hibernia 1808 slp — Thomas 1808 slp — Jane 1811 brg — Mantura 1812 slp — Louisa 1812 ltr — Mars 1813 smk — Shannon 1813 bgn — Venus 1815 sch — Ann 1815 bgn — Betsey 1815 bot — Dove 1816 sch — Mevagissey 1816 bgn — Triumph 1817 sch — Ceres 1820 smk — Maria 1824 sch — Polgooth 1824 sch — Heligan 1830 sch — Cruiser 1831 slp — James Dunn 1833 sch — William Harris 1835 sch — Brilliant 1839 sch — Chronometer 1842 bgn.

FERRIS, Peter, at West Looe at unrecorded date pre-1934.
Moonraker 1934 yht.

FORSYTH, William, at Mevagissey 1812—1814.
Lark 1812 bot — Elizabeth 1812 ltr — Alliance 1814 bgn.

FURSE, James, at Mevagissey 1790.
Unity 1790 slp.

GEACH, William, (The Elder and the Younger) at Polruan 1789—1836.
Betsey 1789 slp — Good Intent 1790 slp — Friendship 1798 bge — Betsey 1800 ctr — Friends Goodwill 1810 ltr — Active 1815 slp — Flower 1816 slp — Good Intent 1818 ltr — Rose 1820 smk — Atlas 1825 slp — Fancy 1825 slp — New House 1825 sch — Happy Return 1826 slp — Lively 1826 slp — St. Austle Packet 1826 slp — Spring 1827 slp — Speculation 1828 sch — Elizabeth & Ann 1829 slp — Charlotte & Hannah 1834 sch — Charlotte Ann 1835 slp — Cornish Trader 1836 slp.

HELLER, Richard, at Fowey 1890.
Rival 1890 kch.

KNIGHT, John, at Charlestown 1839.
Uzella 1839 sch.

LELEAN, Nicholas, (& family) at Mevagissey 1823—1874.
Pembroke 1823 sch — Catherine 1829 sch — Kitty 1830 slp — Freedom 1832 sch — Snowdrop 1833 sch — Joseph & Thomas 1834 slp — Three Sisters 1836 ywl — Julia 1837 sch — Eliza 1837 sch — Lelean 1839 sch

— Elizabeth Mary Ann 1840 sch — John Pearce 1841 bgn — Albion 1846 bgn — Star of the West 1850 lgr — Matilda 1850 lgr — Brenton 1861 sch — Beatrice 1874 sch.

LUKE, Anthony, succeeded by William, at Charlestown 1841—1873.
Engineer 1841 slp — Merchant 1844 bgn — Pentewan 1845 slp — Pet 1848 sch — Jessie 1855 sch — William & Anthony 1862 brg — Maria Louise 1866 sch — Mary Lizzie 1868 sch — Teaser 1868 dandy — Little Fred 1870 smk — Challenge 1870 sch — Pride of the Channel 1873 bgn.

MARKS, John & RENDLE, William, at Polruan, Bodinnick and Fowey 1826—1846.
Abeona 1826 slp — Jane 1826 sch — Selina 1830 sch — William 1831 slp — Success 1834 sch — Penquite 1835 slp — Joan & Mary 1836 slp — Boconnoc 1836 slp — Mount Charles 1837 sch — Lerrin 1838 slp — Louisa 1839 slp — Lady Louisa 1839 slp — Ranger 1839 slp — John & Jenefer 1840 slp — Richard Hicks 1840 sch — Speedwell 1840 sch — Rachael Anne 1841 sch — Lady Eliot 1842 sch — Boscoppa 1842 sch — Unity 1843 sch — Tariff 1844 smk — William West 1846 sch.

MELHUISH, James, at Mevagissey 1787—1804.
Favourite 1787 slp — William & Mary 1788 slp — Happy Go Lucky 1789 slp — Friends 1790 slp — Sally 1791 slp — Alligator 1791 slp — Brothers 1791 slp — Sedwell 1793 slp — Nancy 1793 slp — Active 1793 slp — Ann 1794 slp — Unity 1796 slp — Friendship 1796 slp — Friends Endeavour 1796 slp — Lion 1798 slp — Lion 1798 ctr — Swift 1798 ctr — Betsey 1799 ctr — Brothers 1801 ctr — Betsey 1804 ctr.

MITCHELL, Percy G., at Portmellon 1932—1934.
Ark Royal 1932 yht — Galahad II 1934 yht — Casuarina II 1934 yht.

MOSS, Samuel, at Par 1867—1879.
Lizzie Trenberth 1867 sch — Elizabeth Moss 1869 sch — Julia 1870 sch — Dorothy 1871 sch — Mary Ann 1875 sch — Ada Peard 1875 bgn — Crystal Stream 1877 sch — Ocean Spray 1877 bgn — Bessie Stephens 1878 sch — Samuel Moss 1879 sch.

NICKELS, Thomas, succeeded by George, at Fowey 1786—1865.

Hope 1786 slp — Catherine 1786 slp — Ceres 1789 bgn — Friendly Pilot 1790 slp — Mary 1791 bgn — Friendship 1792 slp — Peggy 1793 slp — Dolphin 1794 lgr — Fowey 1796 bge — Charlotte 1797 bgn — Turbot 1797 slp — Agenoria 1798 slp — Saint Winnow 1798 bge — Fowey 1798 ctr — Betsey 1802 slp — Twins 1803 Shp — Four Brothers 1804 bge — Friends Endeavour 1804 bge — Greyhound 1804 lgr — Peteril 1805 ctr — John & Henry 1805 bge — Alexander 1805 sch — Echo 1806 ctr — Phoebe 1807 bgn — Eagle 1807 bge — Alert 1810 sch — Mary 1811 ltr — Amity 1812 sch — Yeomen's Glory 1813 slp — William & George 1813 ltr — Sceptre 1816 bgn — Amity 1819 ltr — Thomas 1820 bgn — William 1821 sch — Hector 1824 bgn — St. Catharine 1825 sch — William & Amelia 1826 slp — Clio 1827 slp — Margaretta 1828 sch — Eliza Wolseley 1828 slp — Amity 1829 sch — Ann & Elizabeth 1830 sch — Ann 1831 sch — Catharine 1833 sch — Hope 1834 sch — Thomas Prothero 1834 sch — John Hicks 1834 sch — Saracen 1835 sch — Swan 1836 sch — Swift 1836 slp — Place 1836 slp — Richard Jane Ann 1837 slp — Twins 1837 sch — John & Rebecca 1838 sch — Victoria 1838 sch — Sisters 1843 sch - Elizabeth 1845 slp — Ann 1847 ywl — Brilliant 1848 sch — Envoy 1849 ywl — Mary Ann 1849 ywl — Abel 1849 sch — Petrel 1851 slp — Hannah Hicks 1853 brk — Perseverance 1862 bgn — Rosebud 1865 bgn.

PEARCE, Tom and Richard, at Looe 1898—1921.

Moll Flanders 1937 (built 1898) yht — Dauntless 1926 (built 1915) yht — Mollie 1924 (built 1921) yht.

PENGELLY, Abraham, at West Looe 1867.

St. George 1867 sch.

PILL, Richard, at Gorran Haven 1883—1904.

Marjorie 1911 (built 1883) yht — Foye 1904 yht.

POULGRAIN, Richard and Hugh, at Fowey 1811—1817.

Dart 1811 ltr — Good Intent 1814 sch — Good Intent 1817 sch.

RENDLE, William, (see Marks & Rendle).

ROBERTS, Benjamin Harris, succeeded by Henry, at Portmellon and Mevagissey 1864—1909.

Lizzie 1864 sch — Eclat 1865 sch — Secret 1867 lgr — Petrel 1867 lgr — P.M. Willcock 1868 sch — Perseverance 1874 sch — Skirmish 1903 yht — Lintie 1925 (built 1909) yht.

SHAPCOTT, Henry, at Looe 1841—1869.

Diligent 1841 slp — Windsworth 1843 sch — Robert Henry 1847 sch — Ann & Elizabeth 1850 slp — Fanny Buller 1859 sch — John F. Buller 1863 sch — Mayflower (possibly by Pengelly) 1866 sch — Florence 1869 'barquette'.

SHEPHEARD, Thomas, at Mevagissey and Polmear 1786—1810.

Hester 1786 slp — Saint Michael 1786 slp — Saint Michael 1786 slp (a second one) — Fortune 1786 slp — Fortune 1787 lgr — Vigilance 1787 lgr — Venus 1788 slp — Friendship 1789 slp — Sprightly 1789 slp — Sisters 1789 slp — New Fortune 1789 slp — Flora 1790 sch — Ceres 1790 slp — Mary 1790 sch — Speedwell 1790 slp — Nancy 1791 bot — May Flower 1791 slp — Bashful 1791 slp — Mary 1792 slp — Valiant 1793 lgr — Speedwell 1794 lgr — Zephyr 1794 lgr — Hope 1795 slp — Charlestown 1795 bge — Lizard 1795 slp — Fortune 1796 slp — Hawk 1796 slp — Olive 1796 slp — Jane 1796 slp — Lion 1797 slp — Lion 1797 slp (a second one) — Maria 1798 slp — Mars 1798 ctr — Friendship 1798 slp — Speedwell 1798 ctr — Greyhound 1798 ctr — Earl Spencer 1799 ctr — Lion 1799 ctr — Happy Return 1800 ctr — Venus 1800 lgr — Ann 1801 bgn — Neptune 1802 bgn — Samuel 1803 ctr — Union 1803 lgr — Ino 1804 ctr — Dart 1804 ctr — Mary 1804 ctr — Fox 1804 ctr — Mary 1805 ctr — Bee 1805 ctr — Valiant 1805 ctr — Hero 1806 ctr — Betsy 1806 ctr — Susan

1806 ctr — Mars 1807 ctr — Lambe 1809 bgn — Susan 1809 bot — Caledonia 1809 ctr — Kitty 1809 ltr — Industry 1810 ltr.

SLADE, Christopher, succeeded by J. Slade & Sons at Polruan 1856—1929.

Peter & James 1856 bgn — Kate & Ann 1858 sch — Juno 1864 sch — Mary Barrett 1864 sch — Sparkling Wave 1866 sch — Silver Stream 1868 sch — Jane Slade 1870 sch — Snow-flake 1872 sch — Silver Spray 1874 sch — Koh-i-Noor 1877 Bkn — E.S. Hocken 1879 bkn — Foam 1888 yht — Majub 1928 yht — Marie-Louise 1929 yht.

SMITH, Peter, at Mevagissey 1810—1819.

Ann & Elizabeth 1810 slp — Regent 1812 sch — Swiftsure 1812 bgn — Phebe 1813 sch — Union 1815 sch — Eliza 1816 slp — Patty 1818 smk — Mary 1819 sch.

STEPHENS, John, at Charlestown, Fowey and Polruan 1874—1878.

Flying Spray 1874 sch — Ocean Swell 1875 bgn — Little Beauty 1875 sch — Katie Cluett 1876 sch — Spin-away 1877 sch — Emeline Jenkin 1878 sch.

TRESCOWTHICK, John, at Par 1861.

Reformation 1861 kch.

WATTY, William H., at Fowey 1893—1902.

Otter 1893 yht — Airy-Mouse 1894 yht — Water Witch 1899 yht — Rosemary (later named Gladioris, then Cresta) 1902 yht.

WILCOCK, John, at Fowey 1793—1817.

Dolphin 1793 slp — Friends Endeavour 1794 sch — Two Sisters 1796 slp — Industry 1797 slp — Harmony 1798 slp — Friendly Society 1798 slp — Mars 1799 ctr — Industry 1802 ctr — Fortune 1803 ctr — Endeavour 1805 ctr — Providence 1817 ctr.

---

bge = barge, bgn = brigantine, bkn = barquentine, bot = boat, brg = brig, brk = barque, ctr = cutter, kch = ketch, lgr = lugger, lnh = launch, ltr = lighter, sch = schooner, shp = full-rigged ship, smk = smack, yht = yacht, ywl = yawl.

APPENDIX 'G'

'PLANTATION-BUILT' VESSELS REGISTERED AT FOWEY

Name	Place of build and year	Fowey Reg. No. and year	Acquiring owner	Rig	Tons	Demise*
Harriot	Shelburne NS 1786	4/1793	Nickels	sch	13	(Looe —)
John	Harbor Bouchet NS 1828	4/1834	Rolling	sch	85	(Truro 1863)
Mary	Grand Rustico PEI 1815	12/1834	Gaved	sch	67	1838
Aimwell	Hillsborough NBr 1834	2/1838	Pearce	sq rd	155	(Exeter 1839)
Royal Adelaide	Quebec 1831	3/1842	Hicks	brk	410	(Padstow 1869)
Good Intent	Richibucto NBr 1843	2/1843	Hicks	brk	593	1856
James	PEI 1828	8/1844	Keast	sch	58	(Bideford 1867)
Flirt	Cascumpec PEI 1844	14/1846	Harris	sch	64	1849
Anne Elizabeth	Wheatley River PEI 1846	6/1847	Tadd	bgn	118	(Grangemouth 1873)
Rover	New Glasgow PEI 1847	12/1847	Salt	sch	84	1862
St. Andrews	Murray Harbour PEI 1846	1/1848	Hunkin	bgn	115	1877
Margaret	Patamagouche NS 1841	8/1848	Dyer	sch	111	(Teignmouth 1861)
Zuleika	Charlottetown PEI 1848	9/1848	Allen	brg	178	1860
Fortune Teller	PEI 1846	8/1849	Hocken	bgn	110	(Reg. cancelled 1855)
Chase	New Glasgow PEI 1850	3/1851	Hicks	sch	149	1897
Margaret	Grand River PEI 1852	6/1853	Thomas	sch	91	1871
Catherine	PEI 1854	23/1854	Hocken	bgn	130	1877
Lydia	Cascumpec PEI 1855	8/1855	Giles/Dobson	bgn	107	1887
Capella	Pineth PEI 1856	6/1856	Rowett	bgn	123	1888
William	New Glasgow PEI 1857	17/1857	Varcoe	bgn	167	1859
Plover	Pugwash NS 1856	2/1857	Meredith	bgn	111	1871
Polyxena	PEI 1857	4/1858	Hayes	bgn	138	1862
Ossena	PEI 1857	6/1858	Dyer	bgn	150	1887
Concord	PEI 1857	8/1858	Treffry	bgn	143	1884
Phoenix	Montague River PEI 1857	12/1858	Bishop	sch	127	(Llanelly 1864)
Muta	PEI 1859	6/1859	Treffry	sch	76	1864
Carthaginian	PEI 1850	4/1860	Moss	brg	157	(Teignmouth 1871)
George Arkle	Napan NS 1853	5/1861	Dingle	brk	553	(Bridport 1877)
Kingaloch	Wallace NS 1860	9/1861	Dingle	bgn	123	1883
Wild Wave	PEI 1861	15/1861	Hocken	bgn	160	1905
Lady of Port Hill	Port Hill PEI 1861 By Jas. Yeo, Jnr.	17/1861	Curtis	bgn	111	1864
Clio	Wheatley River PEI 1850	2/1862	Perriam	sch	107	1869
James	PEI 1828	8/1862	Skentlebury	sch	56	(Bideford 1867)
Pearl	Hillsboro' River PEI 1852	16/1862	Steele	bgn	107	1863
Hope	PEI 1850	5/1863	Moss	sch	60	1863
Gold	Antigonish NS 1849	2/1864	Harris	bgn	101	(Guernsey 1867)
Little Dorrit	Bedeique PEI 1856	8/1865	Toms	bgn	115	1877
Jane	Crapaud PEI 1866	4/1867	Coombes	bgn	132	(sold foreign 1879)
Isabella Margaret	New Bideford PEI 1864	1/1872	Tadd	bgn	147	1872

Name	Place of build and year	Fowey Reg. No. and year	Acquiring owner	Rig	Tons	Demise*
Sir Robert Hodgson	PEI 1869	3/1872	Parkyn	brg	203	1895
Ontario	Montague PEI 1873	9/1874	Barrett	bgn	167	1884
Fortune	PEI 1875	1/1881	Treffry	bgn	212	1910
Camwood	Mount Stewart PEI (James White) 1877	1/1892	Coode	bgn	125	1896
Raymond (Lady Quirk post 1929)	Summerside PEI (John Lefurgey) 1876	1/1916	Murdoch/ Wilson	bgn	200	(Douglas, Isle of Man c. 1930)

*Transfers to other ports shown in brackets.

Summary:
44 went on the Fowey register. Their average tonnage was 148. 30 of them were square rigged. 13 were subsequently transferred to other ports, 1 was sold foreign, 1 had her register cancelled for an unrecorded reason. 29 were on the register when lost, broken up,. *etc.* and of those the average life was 20 years.

APPENDIX 'H'

MASTERS AND CREWS OF VESSELS REGISTERED AT FOWEY
Midnight December 31 1850

Master's Name	Vessel, Port, No. and Year	Men & Boys Employed
Ashton, William	*Model* 4/1840	4
Ball, James	*Eliza* 24/1837	7
Bartlett, John	*Sally* 1/1808	3
Beale, Thomas W.	*Louisa* 2/1839	4
Bowden, Richard	*Unity* 4/1843	4
Brokenshaw, John	*Touch-me-not* 5/1841	8
Bunt, James	*Speedwell* 8/1840	6
Burton, Richard	*Thomas Prothero* 18/1834	6
Clements, John	*Tariff* 3/1844	4
Climo, John	*Mary Ann & Eliza* 2/1845	4
Climo, Samuel	*Brilliant* 9/1850	4
Climo, William	*New Quay* 10/1847	7
Collins, William	*New House* 22/1825	5
Couch, Edward	*Patty* 10/1818	4
Cornish, Thomas	*United Friends* 5/1843	3
Cross, Thomas	*Star of the West* 1/1850	2
Curtis, William	*Elizabeth & Ann* 4/1829	4
Davey, John	*Ann & Elizabeth* 8/1850	2
Davey, John	*Mary Anna* 8/1846	5
Dobson, George	*Rose* 9/1847	4
Dobson, James	*Ranger* 10/1839	4
Dunn, Joseph	*Three Sisters* 40/1836	2
Dyer, Richard	*John* 7/1826	5
Dyer, Thomas	*William West* 17/1846	5
Ellery, Abraham	*Charlotte & Hannah* 6/1834	5
Ellery, Elijah	*John & Jenefer* 3/1840	4
Ellery, Joseph	*Langurthowe* 7/1837	5
Fowler, Christopher	*Lady Eliot* 9/1842	6
Freeland, George	*Breeze* 6/1846	4
Furse, John	*Chronometer* 1/1842	10
Furse, Joseph	*William Harris* 8/1835	6
George, Thomas	*Richard Carnall* 15/1837	6
Gill, Thomas	*Commerce* 6/1850	2
Glanvill, Joseph	*Catharine* 8/1833	5
Good, William R.	*Elizabeth* 9/1845	5
Graham, William Bell	*Honour* 14/1834	5
Ham, Richard	*Swan* 24/1836	6
Hanson, James	*Enterprise* 11/1846	6
Harvey, Charles R.	*Mary* 18/1846	5
Harvey, Joseph	*Lerrin* 13/1838	4
Hewitt, Thomas	*Pheasant* 8/1815	5
Hicks, John	*Abel* 5/1849	8
Hill, William	*Elizabeth Huddlestone* 7/1850	5
Hine, Thomas R.	*Pet* 12/1848	6
Hingston, James	*Unity* 2/1849	3
Hocken, Edward	*Rachael Ann* 1/1841	5
Hocken, Nathaniel	*Fortune Teller* 8/1849	7
Hocken, William	*John & Rebecca* 3/1838	3
Hodge, Charles	*Engineer* 8/1841	4
Hodge, Roger	*Pentewan* 10/1845	3
Hollow, Richard	*William* 3/1831	4
Holten, Thomas	*Amelia* 9/1849	4
Holten, William	*William* 1/1834	2
Hunkin, John F.	*Pembroke* 3/1823	5
Hunkin, Matthew	*St. Andrews* 1/1848	7
Hunkin, Peter	*Envoy* 1/1849	2
Isbell, John	*Hope* 2/1834	5
James, Robert	*Mary* 6/1849	3
Jenkins, George	*Charlestown* 4/1795	3
Johns, James	*Sophia* 9/1812	5
Johns, Michael	*Mary Ann* 3/1849	3
Johns, Richard	*Eliza* 9/1816	3
Johns, Robert	*Ann* 13/1847	3
Kellow, John	*Mary Ann* 7/1848	3
Kendall, James	*Polgooth* 10/1824	5
Kendall, John	*Saint Catherine* 26/1825	6

Master's Name	Vessel, Port, No. and Year	Men & Boys Employed
Kimbrell, Joseph	Joseph & Thomas 15/1834	2
Lamb, John	Sisters 3/1843	4
Lane, Thomas	Standard 27/1837	4
Lean, Philip	Regent 19/1837	4
Lelean, John	Snowdrop 2/1833	7
Lelean, Richard M.	Lelean 5/1839	6
Lelean, W.B.	Catherine 5/1829	6
Lelean, William	Duporth 10/1811	4
Ley, Thomas	Brilliant 3/1839	6
Ley, Thomas	Freedom 4/1832	6
Libby, John	Need 6/1845	4
Lobb, John R.	Emerald 28/1837	5
Luke, John	Merchant 1/1844	10
Luly, John	John Pearce 9/1841	9
Manley, William H.	Albion 15/1846	9
Mann, William	Boscoppa 11/1842	5
Martyn, Joseph	Margaret 8/1848	6
Melhuish, Thomas	John & Edward 1/1823	6
Melhuish, Thomas Jnr.	Julia 1/1837	6
Moss, Joseph	Good Intent 8/1814	6
Moss, Thomas	Elizabeth 8/1845	4
Nichols, Robert	Hope 5/1845	4
Nickels, Edward	Success 13/1834	6
Nickels, Samuel S.	Amity 3/1829	5
Olive, William J.	Elizabeth Mary Ann 1/1840	8
Pascoe, John	John 3/1841	4
Pascoe, John	Thomas & John 3/1850	3
Pearn, Robert	Charlotte Ann 2/1835	4
Pengelly, Abraham	Reliance 4/1848	7
Pengelly, Benjamin	Union 5/1846	3
Polglase, William	Mount Charles 25/1837	6
Reynolds, Philip	Laurel 5/1832	4
Richards, John	Emerald 1/1820	5
Robins, William	Cork Packet 6/1848	4
Rowe, Charles	John Wesley 10/1848	5
Rowett, Thomas	John Carnall 9/1833	5
Rundell, Henry	Caroline 8/1837	4
Rundle, John	John 3/1841	5
Salt, John	Lavinia 10/1835	3
Salt, John S.	Rover 12/1847	6
Salt, Philip	Alert 6/1842	5
Salt, Philip	Charlotte & Maria 5/1833	4
Sampson, Nicholas	Cornish Trader 1/1836	2
Scantlebury, Thomas	Gallant 9/1839	7
Shapcott, Henry Jnr.	Robert Henry 8/1847	5
Smith, Joseph	John Hicks 11/1834	5
Smith, Richard	Royal Adelaide 3/1842	17
Smith, Richard	Brilliant 2/1848	7
Smith, William	East Cornwall 8/1834	6
Snell, James	Hero 7/1820	3
Stone, William H.	Fancy 8/1825	4
Tadd, James	Bedwelty 7/1841	7
Tadd, John	Eirene 1/1847	5
Tadd, Peter	Sabina 6/1841	6
Tadd, Thomas	Ann Elizabeth 6/1817	7
Tadd, William	Charles Clarke 5/1848	12
Thomas, James	Matilda 2/1850	2
Thomas, John	Tamar 4/1850	3
Tippett, James	Flower 4/1816	3
Toms, William	Par 29/1836	5
Tregaskes, Richard	Ann & Elizabeth 9/1830	5
Trimberth, John	Mary 11/1811	3
Tucker, James	Ant 15/1810	3
Walters, John	James 8/1844	4
Walters, Joseph	Diligent 4/1841	3
Walters, Thomas	Windsworth 1/1843	7
Warburton, John	Good Intent 2/1843	19
Williams, Joseph	Catherine Boland 11/1848	6
Williams, William L.	Zuleika 9/1848	10
Worth, William	Swift 44/1836	3

PRO BT/62/19

APPENDIX 'I'

SUMMARY OF ACCOUNTS FOR BUILDING 149-TON SCHOONER *GALLANT* 1839

		£	s	d
Nicholas Butson	Shipwrights' & Joiners' work	309	7	0
	Cabening, caulking, etc.	40	6	9
	Sawing work	116	16	0
	Making sawpit, kiln, etc.	25	0	0
	Wages & allowances on old work to August 27 1839	46	16	10
John M. Carnall	Sails, etc.	142	1	8
	Oil, twine & other materials	7	5	9½
	?	1	10	4
C. Thomas	Cordage, etc.	163	16	0
Charles Lacey	Blocks, etc. (more than 100 items)	38	16	11
N. Gould	More than 160 items	28	6	5
William Climo	Building work	18	8	3
	Casks, buckets, pails, tubs	6	16	0
Four riggers		12	3	6
William Soady	Windlass apparatus	13	0	0
P. Roberts	Scraping	1	0	0
N. Richards	Pipes, etc.			?
Thomas Bate	Leather			?
		971	11	5½

(*Note:* there appears to be no account for spars)

DD TF 826 Cornwall County Record Office

SCHOONER MAGGIE C

Built at Dysart 1876, 111 tons, registered at Fowey January 9 1877: Voyages, cargoes & cash profits for the 10 years of her life 1877—1887, abstracted from her account-book (in Fowey Town Museum) kept by her managing owner, Captain Nathaniel Crews Stevens Couch.

1877

January 11 to March 1: Dysart with 205 tons of coal — Granville — in ballast — Fowey.

March 1 to April 16: Fowey with 205 tons of china clay — Runcorn.

April 16 to 30: Runcorn with 207 tons of salt — Irvine.

May 1 to 15: Irvine with 200 tons of pig iron — Runcorn.

May 15 to June 15: Runcorn with 220 tons of rock salt — Dort (via Fowey).

June 16 to 30: Dort with pit props — South Alloa.

July 1 to 15: South Alloa with 9 $\frac{4}{10}$ keels of coals — Fecamp.

July 16 to September 15: Fecamp in ballast — Middlesbrough (via Fowey) — with 200 tons of pig iron — Swansea — with 210 tons of coals — Caen (via Falmouth).

September 16 to October 15: Caen in ballast — Fowey — with 212 tons of china stone — Rouen.

October 15 to November 1: Rouen with potatoes — Newport.

November 1 to 30: Newport with 210 tons of coals — Fowey.

December 1 to 31: Fowey with 211 tons of china clay — Millera — with cargo unstated — Fowey.

1878

January 1 to 31: Fowey with potatoes — Newport.

Accounts Summary for 55 weeks January 11 1877 to January 31 1878

	£	s	d
Income	286	10	0
Less disbursements	133	13	10
	152	16	2

or: £2 7s 9d per share for each of 64 shares.

February 1 to 28: Newport with 197 tons of fish plates — Elisy.

March 1 to 15: Elisy with 165 tons of old rails — Stockton-on-Tees.

March 16 to April 15: Stockton-on-Tees — Middlesbrough — with cargo of pipes — St. Michael's Mount, Penzance.

April 16 to 30: Penzance in ballast — Cardiff — with 212 tons of coal — Par.

May 1 to June 15: Par with 215 tons of china clay — Brussels.

June 15 to 30: Brussels with 200 tons of stone — London.

July 1 to 31: London with 160 tons of unstated freight — Portsmouth — in ballast — Charlestown.

August 1 to 31: Charlestown with 214 tons of china clay — Antwerp.

September 1 to 30: Antwerp in ballast to Newcastle-upon-Tyne — with 202 tons of coal — Topsham.

October 1 to 31: Topsham in ballast — Par — with 214 tons of china clay — Rouen.

November 1 to 30: Rouen with unstated cargo — Gloucester.

December 1 to 31: Gloucester in ballast — Newport — with 200 tons of coal — Looe.

Accounts Summary for 48 weeks February 1 to December 31 1878

	£	s	d
Income	166	16	5
Less disbursements	93	6	5
	73	10	0

or: £1 3s per share.

1879

January 1 to 31: Looe with 134 tons of copper — Penarth.

February 1 to 14: Penarth with 207 tons of coals — London.

March 1 to 15: London with 195 tons of manure — Londonderry.

March 15 to 31: Londonderry with general cargo — Ballyness.

April 1 to May 15: Ballyness with ? via Fowey — Ramsgate — Erith — London with 208 tons of iron — Fowey.

May 16 to June 31: Fowey in ballast — Ardrossan — with 203 tons of coals — Plymouth.

July 1 to 31: Plymouth in limestone ballast — Fowey.

August 1 to September 15: Fowey with china stone — Newcastle — with 198$\frac{3}{4}$ tons of coal — Fowey.

September 16 to October 18: Fowey with 216 tons of clay — Rouen.

October 18 to November 15: Rouen with 143 tons 13 cwt of potatoes — Bridgwater via Ilfracombe.

November 15 to December 25: Bridgwater in ballast — Cardiff — 202 tons 19 cwt of coals — Fowey.

December 25 to January 31 1880: Fowey with 210 tons of china clay to Leith.

1880

February 1 to March 15: Leith in ballast to Grimsby and the Humber — 9 keels 3$\frac{3}{4}$ chaldrons of coals — Caen.

Accounts Summary for 62 weeks January 1 1879 to March 15 1880

	£	s	d
Income	205	0	0
Less disbursements	86	1	5$\frac{1}{2}$
	118	18	6$\frac{1}{2}$

or: £1 17s per share.

March 15 to April 15: Caen in ballast — Fowey — 215 tons of china clay — St. Valery.

April 15 to May 15: St. Valery in ballast — Fowey — with 166 tons 22$\frac{1}{2}$ cwt of china clay — Runcorn.

May 15 to June 1: Runcorn with 201 tons 12 cwt of salt — Newcastle.

June 1 to June 30: Newcastle with 186 tons of coals — Paignton.

July 1 to 31: Paignton in ballast — Teignmouth.

August 1 to 26: Teignmouth with 208 tons of china clay — Runcorn.

August 27 to September 26: Runcorn with 193 tons 19 cwt of salt — Newcastle.

September 27 to October 16: Newcastle with 131$\frac{1}{2}$ tons of soda and 69 tons of bricks — London.

October 16 to November 1 — London with 104 tons of carpolites and 90 tons of bones — Newcastle. (*carpolites - fruit converted to stone by silification*).

November 1 to December 10: Newcastle with ? via Grimsby — Caen.

December 11 to January 27 1881: Caen with 135 tons of iron ore — Penarth — with 212 tons of coals — Plymouth — with 60 tons of limestone — Fowey.

Accounts Summary for 45 weeks March 15 1880 to January 27 1881

	£	s	d
Income	155	0	0
Less disbursements	58	17	8
	96	2	4

or: £1 10s per share.

1881

March 1 to 16: Fowey with 213,772 kilos of china clay — Dordt.

March 16 to April 27: Dordt with hoop iron — West Hartlepool — with 200 tons of coal — Dartmouth — in ballast to Fowey.

April 27 to May 26: Fowey with 209½ tons of china clay — Louvain (*sic*).

May 26 to June 13: Louvain (*sic*) with 68 tons of tree bark — Hull.

June 13 to July 13: Hull with 202¾ tons of coals — Plymouth — 80 tons of limestone — Fowey.

Accounts Summary for 20 weeks March 1 to July 16 1881

	£	s	d
Income	95	0	0
Less disbursements	12	17	4
	82	2	8

or: £1 5s 8d per share.

July 16 to August 19: Fowey with 202 tons of china clay — Hamburg.

August 19 to September 19: Hamburg with 218 tons of general cargo — Halsingborg — Halmstad.

September 19 to October 19: Halmstad with 1,012½ quarterns of oats — Gloucester.

October 19 to November 19: Gloucester with ? — Bruges.

November 19 to December 19: Bruges with 195 tons of broken stone — London — with 190 tons 9 cwt of wheat — Bursledon.

December 19 to January 2 1882: Bursledon with old railway chairs — Swansea.

Accounts Summary for 24 weeks July 16 1881 to January 2 1882

	£	s	d
Income	160	1	5½
Less disbursements	31	11	0
	128	10	5½

or: £1 11s 3d per share with £28 10s 5½d carried forward.

1882

January 2 to February 16: Swansea with 205½ tons of coals — Mistley.

February 16 to March 2: Mistley with 591 quarters of wheat — Stockton & Middlesbrough.

March 2 to April 12: Middlesbrough with 201½ tons of pig iron — Swansea.

April 12 to May 2: Swansea with 205 tons of coals — Trouville; in ballast — Fowey.

May 2 to June 7: Fowey with 218,150 kilos of china clay — Antwerp.

June 7 to July 29: Antwerp in ballast — Sunderland; with 191 tons of coals — Salcombe; in ballast — Fowey.

July 29 to September 11: Laid up at Fowey.

September 11 to 29: Fowey with 205½ tons of china clay — Runcorn.

October 1 to 30: Runcorn with 200 775/1000 of salt — Boulogne.

October 30 to December 11: Boulogne with 156 tons 4 cwt of carpolites — Newcastle; with 212 tons of gas coals — Falmouth — Fowey.

Accounts Summary for 52 weeks January 2 to December 31 1882

	£	s	d
Income	219	2	11½
Less disbursements	175	12	6
	43	10	5½

or: 10s per share with £11 10s 5½d carried forward.

1883

January 7 to February 7: Fowey with 214,240 kilos of china clay — Antwerp.

February 7 to 21: Antwerp with 913½ quarters of wheat — London.

February 22 to March 29: London with 284½ tons of Government stores, via Fowey — Haulbowline, Queenstown.

March 29 to April 6: Cork with 278 tons of Government stores — London.

April 7 to May 6: London with 186 tons 16 cwt 24lb of lead ore — Bristol.

May 6 to June 6: Bristol with 207 tons of coals — Fowey.

June 6 to 30: Fowey with 212 tons 2 cwt of china clay — Rotterdam.

July 1 to 15: Rotterdam with paper pulp — Penarth.

July 15 to 31: Penarth with 212 tons of coals — Fowey.

July 31 to August 15: Fowey with 211½ tons of china clay — Rouen.

August 15 to 31: Rouen with 198 tons of gypsum — Plymouth — tow to Fowey.

Accounts Summary for 33 weeks January 7 to August 31 1883

	£	s	d
Income	330	4	1½
Less disbursements	49	12	8
	280	11	5½

or: £4 per share with £24 11s 5½d carried forward.

September 1 to October 6: Fowey with 227,578 kilos of china clay — Rotterdam.

October 6 to November 8: Rotterdam in ballast — South Shields; with 193 tons of coals — Plymouth — Fowey.

November 8 to January 14 1884: Fowey with 250 tons of china clay — Newcastle.

1884

January 14 to February 15: Newcastle with 202 tons of coals — London.

February 15 to March 13: London with 200 tons 6 cwt of patent manure — Clonakilty.

March 13 to April 23: Clonakilty in ballast — Cardiff, with 203 tons of coals — Charlestown.

April 23 to May 23: Charlestown with 205 4/20 tons of china clay — Fleetwood.

May 23 to June 6: Fleetwood with 180 tons of coals — Fowey.

June 6 to July 13: Fowey with 215 tons of china stone — Newcastle.

July 13 to September 1: Newcastle with 199 11/12 tons of coals — Poole.

September 2 to October 1: Poole with 209 tons of blue clay — Glasgow.

October 2 to 20: Glasgow with 205½ tons of coal tar pitch — Cardiff.

October 21 to November 11: Cardiff with 200¹⁵/₂₀ tons of coals — Fowey.

November 11 to December 11: Fowey with 205¹⁰/₂₀ tons of china clay — Boness, Grangemouth.

December 11 to January 31 1885: Grangemouth with pipes — Rochester.

1885

February 1 to March 20: Rochester with 200 tons of cement — Liverpool.

March 20 to April 12: Liverpool with 205 tons of coals — Devonport — tow to Fowey.

April 13 to May 12: Fowey with 181 tons of china clay — Liverpool.

May 13 to June 12: Liverpool with salt — Fowey.

Accounts Summary for 93 weeks September 1 1883 to June 12 1885

	£	s	d
Income	224	11	5½
Less disbursements	102	12	11½
	121	18	6

or: £1 10s per share with £25 18s 6d carried forward.

June 13 to 30: Fowey with 207 tons of clay — Glasgow.

June 30 to July 31: Glasgow with 202 tons 7 cwt of coals — Cardiff.

July 31 to August 17: Cardiff with 202 tons of coals — Greenock.

August 18 to September 10: Brodick Bay (Arran) with 114¹⁸/₂₀ tons of pit coals — Cardiff.

September 10 to 30: Cardiff with 204¹⁷/₂₀ tons of coals — Fowey.

September 30 to October 20: Fowey with 199 tons of china clay — Runcorn.

October 20 to December 31: Runcorn with 116 tons of coals — Fowey.

Accounts Summary for 28 weeks June 12 to December 13 1885

	£	s	d
Income	98	10	7
Less disbursements	24	1	9
	74	8	10

or: £1 per share with £10 8s 10d carried forward.

The following figures appear on this page of the accounts:—

Vessel purchased January 1877 for cash £2,000

				1st year	100		
1878	£1,900			2nd year	95		
1879	£1,805			3rd year	90	5	0
1880	£1,714	15	0	4th year	85	14	9
1881	£1,629	0	3	5th year	81	9	0
1882	£1,547	11	3	6th year	77	7	6
1883	£1,470	5	9	7th year	73	0	3
1884	£1,397	5	6	8th year	69	16	6
1885	£1,327	9	0	9th year	66	7	6
1886	£1,261	1	6	10th year	63	0	0

(Note: Above may be an estimate of the annual decline in the vessel's value from time of purchase to it's loss by collision, possibly for insurance claim purposes. First column of figures appears to be

estimated value, last column the amount by which it had been depreciated, 5% per annum).

1886

January 1 to March 10: At Fowey, laid up, being fitted out.

March 10 to April 30: Fowey with 204 tons of china clay — Runcorn; with 175 tons of coals, 14 tons of salt — Fowey.

April 30 to June 9: Fowey with 214 tons 18 cwt of china clay — Rouen; 194 tons 15 cwt of plaster stone — Plymouth — Fowey.

June 9 to July 17: Fowey — Pentewan with 210¹³/₂₀ tons of china clay — Antwerp.

July 18 to August 31: Antwerp with ground phosphate in bulk — Silloth.

September 1 to 30: Silloth with 185 tons of coals — Fowey.

October 1 to 31: Fowey with 192 tons of china stone — Rouen; towed to Havre.

October 31 to November 14: Havre with 104 tons of sandalwood — Goole.

November 15 to December 26: Goole with 204 tons 4 cwt of seed cake — Plymouth; towed to Fowey.

Accounts Summary for 52 weeks January 1 to December 26 1886

	£	s	d
Income	75	18	11
Less disbursements	64	13	3
	11	5	8

carried forward.

1887

December 1886 to January 26 1887: Fowey with 207 tons of china clay — Maryport.

January 27 to February 26: Maryport with 196 tons of coals — Fowey.

February 27 to March 19: Fowey with 192 tons of china clay — Rouen.

March 20 to April 13: Rouen with 206 tons of plaster stone — London.

April 14 to May 18: London with 75 tons of manure — Cardiff and Newport.

May 19 to June 1887: Newport with 202³/₂₀ tons of coals to Fowey; Fowey (? in ballast) to Cardiff — lost on voyage.

Summary of accounts for 27 weeks December 26 1886 to July 4 1887

	£	s	d
Income	8	7	7½
Less disbursements	30	12	5½
Loss	22	4	10

Cash Profit from Voyages in 9 years and 7 months January 1877 to July 1887:

	£	s	d
55 weeks 11.1.1877—31.1.1878	152	16	2
48 weeks 1.2.1878—31.12.1878	73	10	0
62 weeks 1.1.1879—15.3.1880	118	18	6½
45 weeks 15.3.1880—27.1.1881	96	2	4
20 weeks 1.3.1881—16.7.1881	82	2	8
24 weeks 16.7.1881—2.1.1882	138	10	5½
52 weeks 2.1.1882—31.12.1882	44	10	5½
33 weeks 7.1.1883—31.8.1883	280	11	5½
93 weeks 1.9.1883—12.6.1885	121	18	6

28 weeks 12.6.1885—31.12.1885	74	8	10
52 weeks 1.1.1886—26.12.1886	11	5	8
	£1194	15	1
27 weeks 26.12.1886—4.7.1887, a loss of	22	4	10
Total	£1172	10	3

or: £18.32 per share over the period
or: £1.83 per share per annum
or: a return on the original cost of the vessel (£31.25 per share) of 5.86% per annum.

On July 2 1887 the *Maggie C* was run into in the Bristol Channel by the ss *Dordogne* of Cardiff and sank near Nash Point. Her managing owner appears to have valued her in her tenth year at £1,261, and a claim was settled for £950 plus £23 interest. This, plus balance from voyages, totalled £982; but costs, law expenses, *etc.*, amounted to £117, so that there was a balance due to share among the owners of £865 or £13.50 per share 'in full settlement of all claims and liabilities whatsoever'. This final share-out plus the earnings over the period of £18.32 per share totalled £31.82 which meant that the owners in all received only £0.57 more per share than they had originally paid for the ship.

According to the accounts the final shareholders were:
Captain Nathaniel Crews Stevens Couch,
  managing owner and master . . . . 55 shares
William Vine, Fowey coal merchant . . . . 3 shares
Richard Hellar, Fowey shipwright . . . . 2 shares
Nicholas John Tregaskes, Newport,
  Monmouth, shipbroker . . . . 1 share
R. Barrett, Polruan sailmaker . . . . 1 share
Thomas Mutton, Lerryn timber merchant . . . . 1 share
Mrs. M.A. Lobb (possibly widow of
  John Rawlings Lobb, Fowey
  ship chandler) . . . . 1 share

APPENDIX 'K'

FOWEY *SQUARE RIGGERS OWNED & MANAGED
BY THE HOCKEN FAMILY

VESSEL	Port No. & year	Tons	Rig	Builder	Duration of Hocken interest	Fate
Fortune Teller	8/1849	110	bgn	PEI 1846	1849—1855	reg. cancelled
Catherine	23/1854	130	bgn	PEI 1854	1854—1877	dismantled 1877
Concord	8/1858	133	bgn	PEI 1857	1871—1884	lost 1884
Wild Wave	15/1861	160	bgn	PEI 1861	1861—1896	broken up 1905
Jane & Ann	1/1865	160	bgn	Newburgh, Fife 1864	1865—1893	hulked 1901
Dashing Wave	7/1868	167	bkn	Fife 1868	1868—1892	sunk 1908
Gem	8/1871	164	bgn	Butson Bodinnick 1871	1895—1898	sold 1898
Ocean Traveller	6/1872	199	bkn	Appledore 1872	1872—1878	lost 1878
Maria Luigia	12/1873	131	bgn	Austria 1867	1873—1896	lost 1896
Ada Peard	8/1875	256	bkn	Moss, Par 1875	1875—1915	wrecked 1916
Ocean Ranger	9/1875	281	bkn	Appledore 1875	1875—1904	sold foreign 1916
Ocean Spray	9/1877	267	bkn	Moss, Par 1877	1877—1903	trs. Falmouth 1903
E.S. Hocken	2/1879	296	bkn	Slade, Polruan 1879	1879—1915	abandoned 1917
Gudrun	2/1882	244	bgn	Italy 1874	1882—1888	lost 1892

*The term "square-rigged" was generally applied to a vessel with at least one mast fully square rigged, that is, divided by its standing rigging (and usually physically) into three separate parts from each of which one or more square sails were set on yards. Thus both brigantines and barquentines were correctly spoken of as square rigged. In the administration of the Merchant Shipping Acts in the later nineteenth century, however, a distinction was made in that to take charge of a barquentine clearing from a home port on a passage beyond the limits of the Home Trade a Master had to hold an Ordinary Master's Certificate, entitling the holder to go to sea as the Master of any vessel, steam or sailing, square rigged or fore and aft. A holder of a Master's Certificate of Competence, Fore and Aft, could, however, take charge of a brigantine clearing on a foreign going voyage.

INDEX OF SHIPS

After each name below are the port number and year of each ship's initial register. More than one entry after the same name means that there was more than one vessel of that name. Name changes are indexed under both names. (Name, port number and year of register enable a vessel's particulars

— build, size, rig, owners, fate, etc. — to be found in the Fowey Custom House Ship Register Books). Any subsequent figures are the page numbers of relevant references in this monograph. For the page references to ships not registered at Fowey see the General Index.

CHARLOTTE & ANN 18/1798
CHARLOTTE & HANNAH 6/1834 — 105, 108
CHARLOTTE & MARIA 5/1833 — 105, 109
CHASE 3/1851 — 107: 11/1863
CHRISTIANA CARNALL 2/1851
CHRONOMETER 1/1842 — 105, 108
CLAUSINA 1/1794 — 20: 5/1808
CLIMAX 7/1852
CLIO 3/1827 — 106: 2/1862 — 107
CLODAGH 3/1936
CLOUD 1/1859
CLOWN 3/1859
COMET 1/1873
COMMERCE 19/1806: 6/1850 — 108: 9/1853
CONCORD 8/1858 — 39, 91, 107, 113
CONOID 1/1917 — 64, 76
CONSTANCE 5/1888
CORK PACKET 6/1848 — 109
CORNISH TRADER 1/1836 — 105, 109
CORNUBIA 7/1857
CORNWALL 3/1794
COUNTESS OF JERSEY 4/1881 — 51, 64, 74, 77
COURIER 17/1806
CRESTA 3/1902 — 106
CRUISER 10/1831 — 105
CRYSTAL STREAM 4/1877 — 89, 105
DARING 2/1890 — 64
DART 13/1803: 17/1804 — 106: 14/1811 — 106: 10/1819: 15/1854
DASHING WAVE 7/1868 — 39, 51, 89, 113
DAUNTLESS 2/1926 — 106
DEERHOUND 4/1898 — 63, 65, 74
DEFENCE 28/1786
DEFIANCE 9/1788
DELABOLE 11/1871
DEVONIA 1/1895 — 89
DIANA 3/1926
DICK & HARRY 1/1814: 6/1817
DICKINS 6/1830
DILIGENCE 3/1793 — 14
DILIGENT 4/1841 — 106, 109
DOLPHIN 8/1792: 13/1793 — 106: 4/1794 — 106: 9/1795
DOROTHY 2/1871 — 89, 105
DOROTHY LOU 1/1926
DOVE 5/1816 — 105
DUKE OF WELLINGTON 9/1815 — 31
DUNLEARY 1/1933 — 87
DUPORTH 10/1811 — 109
EAGLE 4/1790 — 18: 22/1807 — 106
EARL CAIRNS 2/1917 — 77, 80, 81: re-registered 3/1929

EARL SPENCER 8/1799 — 106
EAST CORNWALL 8/1834 — 105, 109
EASTMORA 3/1939
EBOR 5/1898
ECHO 15/1806 — 106: 20/1806
ECLAT 9/1865 — 106
EDMUND 3/1834
EDWARD 11/1810
EIRENE 1/1847 — 109
ELIZA 21/1806: 9/1816 — 106, 108: 24/1837 — 105, 108
ELIZA ANNIE 13/1866
ELIZA HANSON 16/1852 — 105
ELIZA WOLSELEY 9/1828 — 106
ELIZABETH 19/1786: 18/1811: 15/1812 — 105: 6/1827: 9/1828: 8/1845 — 109: 9/1845 — 106, 108
ELIZABETH ANN 6/1811
ELIZABETH & ANN 4/1829 — 105, 108
ELIZABETH & GRACE 7/1823
ELIZABETH & JANE 3/1815
ELIZABETH DAVEY 5/1856
ELIZABETH HILL 3/1863 — 89
ELIZABETH HUDDLESTON 7/1850 — 108
ELIZABETH JANE 1/1887
ELIZABETH MARY ANN 1/1840 — 105, 109
ELIZABETH MOSS 1/1869 — 89, 105
ELLEN FRANCIS 6/1855
ELLIN LLOYD 2/1912
EMBLEM 1/1851
EMBLYN 1/1888
EMELINE JENKIN 1/1878 — 53, 54, 89, 106
EMERALD 1/1820 — 105, 109: 28/1837 — 109
EMILIE DINGLE 7/1876
EMILY ELLEN 7/1872 — 36, 52
EMPRESS 1/1864
ENDEAVOUR 15: 43/1787: 7/1788: 4/1792: 7/1794: 4/1797: 8/1803: 19/1805 — 106
ENGINEER 8/1841 — 105, 108
ENTERPRISE 11/1846 — 105, 108
ENTERPRIZE 1/1807
ENVOY 1/1849 — 106, 108
E S HOCKEN 2/1879 — 36, 37, 51, 52, 60, 65, 68, 76, 96, 106
EXCELLENT 3/1832 — 105
EXHIBITION 11/1852
EXPECTATION 29/1786: 12/1797

EXPERIMENT 18/1786 — 21
FAME 25/1807 — 105: 10/1870
FANCY 26/1786: 8/1825 — 47, 48, 49, 58, 105, 109: 3/1910 — 77
FAN-KWAE 4/1884
FANNY 11/1816: 3/1855
FANNY BULLER 4/1859 — 55, 106
FAVOURITE 35/1787 — 14: 37/1787 — 105: 11/1789 — 20
FERONIA 14/1873
FERRET 18/1803 — 10
FHC No. 1 3/1924
FHC No. 2 1/1924
FHC No. 3 4/1924
FHC No. 4 5/1924
FHC No. 5 6/1924
FHC No. 6 2/1925
FHC No. 7 1/1936
FIVE BROTHERS 18/1793 — 14
FLIRT 2/1803: 14/1846 — 107
FLORA 5/1790 — 20, 106: 12/1796: 1/1801 — 20: 10/1840
FLORENCE 89: 4/1855: 13/1869 — 35, 54, 106: 4/1873 — 77
FLOWER 4/1816 — 105, 109
FLOWER GIRL 5/1876
FLY 18: 5/1797 — 20: 5/1801 — 20: 7/1807: 6/1815
FLYING SPRAY 8/1874 — 53, 54, 106
FOAM 3/1888 — 77, 87, 106
FORAGER 6/1854 — 41, 42
FORTUNATE 7/1874 — 94
FORTUNE 15: 24/1786: 32/1786 — 20, 106: 36/1787 — 106: 2/1796 — 106: 22/1803 — 106: 22/1804: 4/1806: 1/1881 — 94, 95, 108
FORTUNE TELLER 8/1849 — 39, 107, 108, 113
FOUR FRIENDS 1/1831
FOUR BROTHERS 47/1787: 7/1804 — 106
FOUR SISTERS 4/1805 — 14: 24/1824
FOWEY 15: 15/1876: 3/1795 — 13: 10/1796 — 106: 3/1798: 13/1798 — 106: 3/1808: 10/1810: 7/1812 — 25
FOX 24/1804 — 106: 3/1811
FOY 5/1902 — 63, 65, 74, 77
FOYE 3/1904 — 73, 74, 77, 106
FRANCES 15/1862 — 94
FRANCIS & MARY 12/1807
FRAU MINNA PETERSEN 3/1901 — 75, 82, 90

FREDERIC WILLIAM 13/1863
FREEDOM 4/1832 — 105, 109
FRIENDLY PILOT 1/1790 — 106
FRIENDLY SOCIETY 7/1798 — 106
FRIENDS 15/1790 — 105: 14/1810:
    8/1853
FRIENDS' ENDEAVOUR 6/1794 — 25,
    106: 13/1796 — 105: 16/1804 — 106:
    7/1805
FRIENDS' GOODWILL 5/1786: 11/1791:
    5/1810 — 105
FRIENDSHIP 8/1788: 1/1789 — 106:
    15/1792 — 106: 7/1796 — 105: 11/1798
    — 105: 14/1798 — 106: 3/1854: 6/1864
GALAHAD II 2/1934 — 94, 105
GALLANT 9/1839 — 31, 32, 96, 105, 109:
    1/1884 — 51, 64, 74, 77, 92
GAME COCK 1/1930
GARLAND 5/1791 — 20
GEM 8/1871 — 56, 60, 65, 105, 113
GENERAL DOYLE 24/1807
GENERAL SMALL 7/1795
GEORGE 7/1816 — 105
GEORGE ARKLE 5/1861 — 40, 97, 107
GEORGE'S 8/1806
G H BEVAN 8/1890 — 77
GIPSEY 2/1873
GIPSY 7/1858: 5/1899
GITANA 7/1867
GLADORIS 3/1902 — 106
GLEANER 2/1827 — 105: 7/1877
GOLD 2/1864 — 107
GOOD INTENT 2/1790 — 105: 8/1814 —
    106, 109: 5/1817 — 106: 3/1818 — 105:
    6/1835: 2/1843 — 40, 42, 97, 107, 109
GRACE 16/1798: 26/1802: 3/1804
GRACIAN 1/1932 — 105
GREYHOUND 19/1798 — 106: 5/1804:
    23/1804 — 106: 6/1806
GRIFFIN 4/1844
GRIMALDI 1/1862
GUDRUN 2/1882
HAFOD 2/1868
HANNAH 6/1798: 14/1854 — 89
HANNAH HICKS 10/1853 — 106
HAPPY GO LUCKEY 10/1789 — 105
HAPPY RETURN 7/1800 — 15, 106:
    6/1826 — 105
HAPPY SOCIETY 12/1800 — 14
HARMONY 5/1798 — 106
HARRIET 9/1819
HARRIET WILLIAMS 5/1880 — 76

HARRIOT 9/1786 — 24: 4/1793 — 29,
    107: 7/1818 — 105
HARRIOT & MATILDA 12/1808
HARVEST MAID 3/1877
HAWK 8/1796 — 21, 106
HECTOR 3/1824 — 106
HEED 12/1804: 9/1813 — 105: 17/1824
HELENA ANNA 3/1892 — 1, 77, 86, 89, 92
HELIGAN 1/1830 — 105
HENDRA 10/1801 — 6
HENRIETTA & NANCY 9/1826
HENRY 16/1824: 20/1824 — 105
HENRY & MARGARET 9/1864
HERO 7/1793 — 21: 9/1806 — 106:
    7/1820 — 31, 109
HESTER 10/1786 — 106
HIBERNIA 6/1808 — 105
HIRAM 29/1802 — 105
HONORAH 5/1910
HONOUR 13/1834 — 105, 108
HOPE 15: 1/1786 — 20, 106: 20/1786:
    2/1795 — 106: 25/1802: 6/1804:
    13/1808: 8/1813: 2/1834 — 106, 108:
    5/1845 — 109: 5/1863 — 107
HYDRA 10/1830 — 31
HYLTON 5/1851
ICHNEUMON 2/1933 — 105
IDA 2/1807
IDEA 1/1811
I'LL AWAY 8/1864 — 89
IMOGENE 2/1906
INCREASE 48/1787
INDEFATIGABLE 16/1810
INDUSTRY 27/1786: 2/1797 — 106: 24/1802 —
    106: 6/1810 — 106: 2/1819: 8/1839: 7/1889 —
    77
INO 8/1804 — 106: 3/1810
ISABEL 1/1919 — 1, 77, 92
ISABELLA 3/1865 — 4, 36, 52, 69, 70, 89
ISABELLA MARGARET 1/1872 — 107
ISLAND MAID 3/1886 — 64
JAMES 9/1820: 8/1844 — 107, 109: 8/1862 —
    107
JAMES & ANN 6/1805
JAMES & ELIZABETH 12/1798: 10/1834
JAMES DUNN 3/1833 — 105
JANE 14/1796 — 10, 106: 9/1801: 1/1803:
    15/1805: 23/1806 — 105: 12/1811 — 105:
    8/1826 — 105: 7/1835: 8/1862: 4/1867 — 52,
    107
JANE & ANN 1/1865 — 39, 113
JANE BANKS 3/1901 — 1, 77, 82, 86, 89, 90, 91

JANE & ELIZABETH 1/1813
JANE KILGOUR 4/1892
JANE SLADE 5/1870 — 59, 60, 77, 96, 106
JANIE GOUGH 4/1890
JANIE MORCOM 11/1865
JASPER 5/1884
JEMIMA 10/1809
JENNY (or PENNY) 7/1786: 38/1787
JESSIE 5/1855 — 105: 7/1901 — 76
JESSIE BENNET 8/1889
JOAN 3/1891
JOAN & MARY 51/1836 — 105
JOANNA 6/1786
JOBSON 13/1812
JOHANNA 8/1810 — 14
JOHN 7/1826 — 108: 4/1834 — 107: 3/1841 —
    109
JOHN & EDWARD 1/1823 — 109
JOHN & HENRY 14/1805 — 106
JOHN & JENEFER 3/1840 — 105, 108
JOHN & MARY 2/1788
JOHN & REBECCA 3/1838 — 106, 108
JOHN CARNALL 9/1833 — 105, 109
JOHN CLARK 1/1863: 1/1871 — 89
JOHN FARLEY 12/1864 — 89
JOHN F BULLER 12/1863 — 106
JOHN HICKS 11/1834 — 106, 109
JOHN PARDEW 2/1878
JOHN PEARCE 9/1841 — 105, 109
JOHN WESLEY 10/1848 — 105, 109
JOHN WILLIAM 8/1811
JOSEPH 5/1795: 13/1831
JOSEPH & THOMAS 15/1834 — 105, 109
JUBILEE 13/1809 — 34: 19/1834
JULIA 1/1837 — 105, 109: 4/1870 — 51, 105
JUNO 7/1864 — 106
KATE & ANNE 2/1858 — 106
KATIE CLUETT 4/1876 — 53, 54, 75, 76, 106
KINGALOCH 9/1861 — 107
KITTY 12/1809 — 106: 5/1830 — 105
KITTY & CLARA 14/1816 — 105
KOH-I-NOOR 5/1877 — 52, 60, 65, 106
L73 2/1939
LADY ELIOT 9/1842 — 105, 108
LADY ERNESTINE 3/1873
LADY FITZGERALD 11/1824
LADY LOUISA 7/1839 — 105
LADY OF PORT HILL 17/1861 — 107
LAMBE 5/1809 — 106
LAMORNA 1/1870
LANGURTHOWE 7/1837 — 31, 32, 108
LARK 12/1812 — 105: 1/1861: 5/1864

LAUNCESTON 3/1878
LAUREL 5/1832 — 105, 109
LAVINIA 10/1835 — 105, 109
LEADER 13/1877
LELEAN 5/1839 — 105, 109
LERRIN 13/1838 — 105, 108
LEVANT STAR 4/1835
LILLAH 2/1938
LILLY 15/1803
LILY 17/1805: 2/1895
LINTIE 1/1925 — 106
LION 3/1797 — 106: 9/1797 — 106: 8/1798 —
    18, 19, 105: 10/1798 — 105: 10/1799 — 106
LITTLE BELLE 3/1898 — 94, 95
LITTLE BEAUTY 7/1875 — 53, 54, 106
LITTLE DORRIT 8/1865 — 107: 3/1887
LITTLE FRED 2/1870 — 105
LITTLE GEM 1/1893 — 64, 76, 89
LITTLE GIPSY 2/1932 — 94, 105
LITTLE JOHN 12/1813
LITTLE LIZ 11/1853
LITTLE MINNIE 1/1891
LITTLE MYSTERY 5/1887 — 52, 64, 76, 89
LITTLE PAL 1/1915 — 77
LITTLE PET 4/1888 — 52, 62, 89, 105
LITTLE PUZZLE 2/1893
LITTLE SECRET 6/1887 — 76
LITTLE WONDER 2/1886 — 52, 64
LIVELY 10/1792 — 21: 2/1800: 20/1804:
    4/1809: 3/1813: 10/1826 — 105
LIZARD 10/1795 — 106
LIZZIE 3/1864 — 77, 106
LIZZIE TRENBERTH 6/1867 — 54, 55, 77,
    89, 105
LORD NELSON 4/1800 — 20, 105
LOTTERY 9/1805 — 10, 20
LOUISA 14/1812 — 105: 2/1839 — 41, 46,
    105
LOUISE CHARLOTTE 6/1876
LOVE 7/1802: 31/1802
LUCY 2/1820 — 31
LURLINE 4/1861
LUSHINGTON 16/1802
LYDIA 8/1807: 8/1855 — 107
LYDIA CARDELL 16/1873 — 36, 77, 82,
    85, 89, 95
MAGGIE C 1/1877 — 47, 48, 49, 96, 110,
    111, 112, 113
MAJUB 2/1928 — 87, 106
MAKERA 4/1933 — 105
M'AIME 3/1881
MANDARA 1/1901

MANTURA 4/1812 — 105
MARGARET 8/1848 — 107, 109: 6/1853
    — 107: 7/1854
MARGARETTA 3/1828 — 106
MARIA 2/1798 — 106: 3/1800: 9/1808:
    3/1812: 7/1824 — 105: 2/1894 — 76, 86
MARIA LOUISE 12/1866 — 42, 105
MARIA LUIGIA 12/1873 — 91, 113
MARIA STUART 11/1862
MARIE-LOUISE 1/1929 — 87, 106
MARINER 16/1806
MARIS STELLA 4/1889
MARJORIE 5/1911 — 77, 106
MARS 9/1798 — 9, 106: 6/1799 — 106:
    21/1807 — 106: 7/1813 — 14, 105
MARSHAL BLUCHER 4/1827
MARSHALL KEITH 3/1889
MARTHA 1/1797: 9/1800: 4/1862
MARTHA EDMONDS 8/1878 — 74, 76
MARY 15: 33/1787: 8/1790 — 106:
    9/1790 — 24: 1/1791 — 106: 13/1792
    — 106: 13/1794: 7/1797: 15/1802 —
    20, 105: 22/1802: 21/1804 — 106:
    5/1805 — 106: 11/1808: 11/1811 —
    106, 109: 8/1819 — 106: 12/1834 —
    107: 18/1846 — 108: 6/1849 — 108:
    15/1853: 17/1853: 17/1854: 1/1858:
    18/1861
MARY & BETSEY 1/1800: 4/1802
MARY & ELIZABETH 8/1797
MARY & MARTHA 11/1803
MARY ANN 12/1794: 23/1803 — 14:
    13/1810: 11/1812: 7/1848 — 108:
    3/1849 — 106, 108: 1/1875 — 89, 105:
    5/1886
MARY ANNA 8/1846 — 108: 4/1863
MARY ANN & ELIZA 2/1845 — 47, 49,
    108
MARY BARRETT 11/1864 — 106
MARY FARLEIGH 10/1871
MARY HELEN 14/1857
MARY JANE 2/1861
MARY JOHNS 7/1887
MARY KELLOW 5/1862
MARY LIZZIE 4/1868 — 105
MARY MILLER 1/1935 — 64, 85, 86, 89,
    92
MARY OGLE 10/1861
MARY PEERS 5/1921 — 72, 81
MARY SANDERS 10/1863
MATCHLESS 6/1807: 11/1854
MATILDA 2/1850 — 105, 109

MAY FLOWER 10/1791 — 106: 6/1813
MAYFLOWER 7/1866 — 106
MEANDER 7/1933 — 94
MELODY MAID 2/1933 — 105
MERCHANT 1/1844 — 105, 109
MERIDIAN 24/1854
MERSEY 9/1866
M D SARAH 3/1860
METEOR 2/1898
MEVAGISSEY 15/1816 — 105
MINA 2/1929
MINERVA 11/1795
MODEL 4/1840 — 31, 32, 105, 108
MOLL FLANDERS 1/1937 — 106
MOLLIE 7/1924 — 106
MONARCH 1/1902
MOONRAKER 1/1934 — 105
MOUNT CHARLES 25/1837 — 105, 109
MUNGO 2/1884
MUTA 6/1859 — 107
MYSTERY 12/1853
NANCY 39/1787 — 18, 20: 3/1790:
    6/1791 — 106: 3/1792: 2/1793 — 105:
    8/1793
NANCY & MARY 15/1809
NATASHA 3/1938
NATAL 8/1877 — 35
NATSOPA 3/1937 — 105
NAVIGATION 2/1804
NEED 6/1845 — 105, 109
NEREID 1/1896
NEPTUNE 20/1802 — 18, 106
NETTLE 4/1810
NEW EXPECTATION 3/1799
NEW HOUSE 22/1825 — 105, 108
NEW FORTUNE 12/1789 — 18, 106
NEW QUAY 23/1786: 10/1847 — 31, 108
NICHOLAS 5/1793
NORDKAP 3/1876
NORMA 3/1899 — 63, 65, 97
OCEAN 5/1854
OCEAN RANGER 9/1875 — 36, 38, 51,
    67, 68, 96, 113
OCEAN SPRAY 9/1877 — 35, 36, 51, 66,
    68, 105, 113
OCEAN SWELL 6/1875 — 53, 54, 65, 76,
    81, 93, 94, 95, 106
OCEAN TRAVELLER 6/1872 — 51, 52,
    113
OCEAN WAVF 11/1870 — 76
OLIVE 9/1796 — 106
OLIVE BRANCH 9/1889

ONE & ALL 52/1836 — 34, 105
ONTARIO 9/1874 — 108
OPAL 2/1930
OPORTO 13/1864
ORCHID 1/1926
OSSENA 6/1858 — 107
OTTER 4/1893 — 77, 106
PALACE 6/1816
PAMELA 2/1818
PANOPE 7/1856
PAR 29/1836 — 31, 109: 2/1902 — 63, 65, 74
PARR PIER 9/1831
PASS BY 3/1885 — 64
PATIENCE 7/1799: 5/1814
PATRA 2/1901
PATTY 10/1818 — 106, 108
PEARL 6/1800 — 105: 16/1862 — 107
PEDESTRIAN 10/1877 — 77, 89
PEGGY 22/1786: 10/1793 — 106: 6/1801
PEGGY & BETSEY 2/1805
PEMBROKE 3/1823 — 105, 108: 4/1901
PENDENNICK 1/1930 — 92
PENDRAGON 4/1926 — 105
PENLEATH 1/1927 — 92
PENNY (or JENNY) 7/1786
PENQUITE 1/1835 — 39, 105
PENSILVA 4/1899
PENTEWAN 10/1845 — 103, 108
PERSEVERANCE 11/1802: 11/1807: 12/1862 – 106: 2/1863: 3/1874 – 53, 76, 89, 91, 106
PET 12/1848 — 105, 108
PETERIL 10/1805 — 106
PETER & JAMES 4/1856 — 58, 106
PETREL 8/1851 — 106: 5/1867 — 106
PHEASANT 13/1811: 8/1815 — 108: 18/1836
PHEBE 4/1813 — 14, 106
PHOEBE 16/1807 — 106
PHENIX 2/1791
PHOENIX 18: 13/1786: 46/1787: 12/1858 — 107
PINK 13/1804
PIONEER 3/1884
PLACE 12/1819 — 105: 50/1836 — 34, 106
PLATINA 2/1853 — 35, 97
PLOUGH 9/1862
PLOVER 2/1857 — 107
PLYMOUTH 14/1801 — 105
P M WILLCOCK 1/1868 — 106
POLDHU 1/1939 — 92, 97
POLGOOTH 10/1824 — 105, 108
POLLY & EMILY 1/1907 — 64
POLPERRO 1/1938 — 92, 97

POLYXENA 4/1858 — 107
POMONA 11/1792: 6/1793 — 21: 10/1800
PRIDE OF THE CHANNEL 8/1873 — 105
PRINCE OF WALES 15/1791 — 14
PRINCESS ALEXANDRA 6/1863
PRINCESS HELENA 12/1874
PROSPER 13/1813
PROSPEROUS MARY 12/1793 — 10
PROVIDENCE 42/1787: 8/1789: 7/1806 — 36: 4/1808: 8/1817 — 106
RACER 5/1866 — 42
RACHAEL ANNE 1/1841 — 39, 47, 49, 105, 108
RANGER 14/1802: 1/1805 — 105: 10/1839 — 105, 108
RASHLEIGH 8/1802: 18/1802 — 18
RAYMOND 1/1916 — 77, 108
RAYONETTE 2/1884
REBECCA 15/1807 — 14: 7/1862 — 105
RECOVERY 6/1788
RED ROVER 8/1860
REDSTART 1/1906
REFORMATION 7/1861 — 106
REGENT 5/1812 — 106: 19/1837 — 109
RELIANCE 4/1848 — 109
RENOWN 3/1805: 11/1806
RESOLUTE 6/1890
RESOLUTION 30/1786: 10/1803
RESTLESS 4/1880
RESTLESS OF PLYNN 2/1937
REWARD 45/1787 — 20
RHODA 4/1864
RICHARD & ELIZABETH 25/1824
RICHARD & JANE 2/1829 — 65, 105: 3/1868 — 77
RICHARD CARNALL 15/1837 — 105, 108
RICHARD HICKS 9/1840 — 105
RICHARD JANE ANN 6/1837 — 106
RIDGWAY 1/1927
RIPPLING WAVE 6/1869 — 44, 45, 56, 89, 105
RIVAL 1/1890 — 60, 73, 77, 84, 89, 105
ROBERT HENRY 8/1847 — 106, 109
ROB THE RANTER 2/1885
ROSA 1/1901
ROSE 4/1799 — 20, 105: 10/1808: 5/1820 — 105: 9/1847 — 108
ROSEBUD 4/1865 — 106
ROSEMARY 3/1902 — 77, 106
ROSE OF TORRIDGE 2/1883
ROTHIEMAY 6/1899
ROVER 19/1810: 12/1847 — 107, 109: 1/1882
ROYAL ADELAIDE 3/1842 — 42, 43, 97, 107, 109
ROYAL TAR 1/1894

RTK 9/1863 — 89
RUBY 1/1904 — 76
SABINA 6/1841 — 105, 109
ST ANDREWS 1/1848 — 107, 108
ST AUSTELL 13/1873
ST AUSTLE 5/1823
ST AUSTLE PACKET 12/1826 — 105
ST CATHARINE 26/1825 — 106, 109
ST GEORGE 3/1867 — 55, 106: 5/1873
ST GERMANS 3/1898 — 94, 95
ST IVES 11/1818
SAINT AUSTLE 16/1786
SAINT MICHAEL 11/1786 — 18, 106: 31/1786 — 106: 2/1789
SAINT WINNOW 4/1798 — 106
SALLY 8/1791 — 105: 23/1807: 1/1808 — 28, 29, 108
SAMSON 1/1900
SAMUEL 7/1803 — 106
SAMUEL MOSS 1/1879 — 105
SARACEN 5/1835 — 106
SARAH 2/1887 — 64
SARAH ANN 2/1856 — 76
SARAH FOX 5/1869
SARAH LIGHTFOOT 2/1897 — 86, 89
SCEPTRE 12/1803: 2/1816 — 106
SEA GULL 1/1857
SEA MAIDEN 1/1932 — 105
SECRET 1/1867 — 106
SEDWELL 1/1793 — 105
SELINA 2/1830 — 105
SELINA ANN 10/1862
SEVEN BROTHERS 16/1801 — 14, 20
S F PEARCE 2/1924 — 82, 86, 92
SHAHEEN 6/1932 — 105
SHAMROCK 7/1860
SHANNON 11/1813 — 105
SHEILING 1/1913
SHEPHERDESS 2/1891 — 64
SILENCE 10/1865
SILVERLANDS 6/1878
SILVER SPRAY 5/1874 — 106
SILVER STREAM 5/1868 — 106
SILVIA 2/1915 — 76
SIR ROBERT HODGSON 3/1872 — 108
SIR SIDNEY SMITH 7/1809
SISTERS 8/1786: 1/1788: 5/1789 — 106: 4/1807: 4/1822 — 31: 6/1823: 3/1843 — 106, 109
SKIRMISH 1/1903 — 64, 65, 73, 74, 77, 106
SMEW 4/1934 — 105
SNOWDROP 2/1833 — 105, 109
SNOW-FLAKE 4/1872 — 106

SOCIETY 14/1793
SOPHIA 16/1793 — 14: 9/1812 — 108
SPARKLE 1/1905 — 64, 73, 74
SPARKLING FOAM 3/1915
SPARKLING WAVE 14/1866 — 52, 106
SPARROW 4/1818: 1/1826
SPECULATION 14/1804: 2/1828 — 105
SPECULATOR 13/1800 — 21
SPEEDWELL 10/1790 — 106: 2/1794 — 10, 12, 106: 6/1795 — 21: 17/1798 — 106: 19/1802 — 10: 20/1803: 8/1840 — 105, 108
SPIN-AWAY 11/1877 — 53, 54, 76, 106
SPINDRIFT 1/1911
SPRAY 5/1936
SPRIGHTLY 3/1789 — 106: 9/1789: 4/1819
SPRING 1/1827 — 105: 4/1886 — 64
STAG 5/1802
STANDARD 27/1837 — 31, 40, 105, 109
STAR OF THE WEST 1/1850 — 105, 108
STERLING 5/1881 — 86
STOCKTON 1/1897 — 63, 65
SUCCESS 3/1807: 13/1834 — 105, 109
SUCCESSFUL 5/1872
SUSAN 18/1806 — 106: 9/1809 — 106: 22/1854
SUSANNA 34/1787: 11/1801: 4/1821 — 31
SWALLOW 23/1802: 14/1807
SWAN 6/1819: 3/1822: 24/1836 — 106, 108
SWEET HOME 4/1932 — 105
SWIFT 20/1798 — 105: 2/1799 — 9, 20: 6/1803: 25/1804: 44/1836 — 106, 109: 12/1877
SWIFTSURE 10/1812 — 106
TAGUS 7/1831
TALARVOR 1/1883
TAMAR 4/1850 — 109
TARIFF 3/1844 — 105, 108
TEAL 1/1915
TEASER 6/1868 — 105
TEATS HILL 17/1834
TELEGRAM 16/1857
TEMPTRESS 4/1910
THAMES 13/1857: 1/1923
THEODORA 4/1894 — 77
THETIS 9/1873 — 48, 57, 58, 105
THOMAS 2/1808 — 12: 14/1808 — 105: 10/1820 — 106: 5/1831: 12/1857
THOMAS AYLAN 2/1860 — 56, 77, 86, 105

THOMAS & JOHN 3/1850 — 109: 8/1856
THOMAS PROTHERO 18/1834 — 106, 108
THOMAS VARCOE 1/1856
THREE FRIENDS 3/1791
THREE SISTERS 40/1836 — 105, 108
TIMES 14/1803
TITANIA 2/1913 — 64, 77
TON MAWR 5/1875
TORFREY 3/1900 — 63, 65, 74
TOUCH-ME-NOT 5/1841 — 52, 56, 105, 108
TRAVELLER 6/1901 — 77, 86, 89
TREFFRY 7/1870 — 49, 50, 51, 64, 74, 77, 87
TREGEAGLE 1/1922
TREVELLAS 1/1918 — 77, 81
TREWARTHA 6/1852 — 47
TRIO 1/1854
TRIUMPH 7/1817 — 105
TRUE BLUE 13/1790
TRUSTY 2/1904
TRUTH 14/1852
TRYPHENA 8/1872
TURBOT 10/1797 — 106
TWINKLE 1/1913 — 73, 74, 77, 94
TWINS 19/1803 — 13, 106: 16/1837 — 106
TWO BROTHERS 14/1786: 25/1786: 5/1788: 6/1792: 11/1794: 16/1816: 11/1825 — 31: 4/1845
TWO FRIENDS 10/1802
TWO SISTERS 17/1793: 6/1796 — 106: 3/1830
UDNEY 2/1881 — 73
UNDINE 4/1875 — 35, 57, 105
UNION 5/1800: 9/1803 — 106: 5/1811: 7/1815 — 106: 8/1820 — 31: 5/1846 — 109
UNION PACKET 4/1823 — 105
UNITED FRIENDS 1/1809: 5/1843 — 108
UNITY 6/1790 — 105: 3/1796 — 105: 24/1803: 19/1807: 9/1811: 4/1843 — 105, 108: 2/1849 — 108: 9/1854
UZELLA 1/1839 — 105: 15/1857
VALIANT 9/1793 — 106: 21/1805 — 106
VENUS 36: 3/1788 — 20, 106: 11/1800 — 106: 17/1802: 28/1802 — 105: 18/1807: 1/1815 — 105: 8/1828 — 31, 32
VERTUMNUS 1/1795: 11/1797 — 14, 105
VESPER 9/1867
VICTORIA 14/1838 — 106: 6/1889

VICTORY 2/1876
VIDA 7/1890
VIGILANCE 40/1787 — 106: 11/1790 — 18, 20
VIGILANT 4/1796
VIRTUOUS GRACE 4/1804 — 14
VISION 6/1857
VIXEN 2/1889
VOLUNTEER 1/1889 — 86
W31 2/1936
WANDERER 8/1852
WATERLILY 10/1866
WATERLOO 10/1816
WATER WITCH 2/1899 — 77, 106
WATERWITCH 2/1918 — 1, 52, 68, 77, 81, 82, 83, 86, 89, 90, 94, 95
WAVE 8/1876
W E GLADSTONE 1/1914 — 77
WEGRAS 2/1939
WHITE FOX II 3/1933 — 105
WILD WAVE 15/1861 — 39, 91, 107, 113
WILLIAM 14/1792: 3/1806: 6/1809: 5/1821 — 106: 3/1831 — 105, 108: 1/1834 — 108: 17/1857 — 107: 2/1900
WILLIAM & AMELIA 11/1826 — 106
WILLIAM & ANN 4/1852
WILLIAM & ANTHONY 14/1862 — 105
WILLIAM & GEORGE 10/1813 — 106
WILLIAM & MARY 4/1788 — 105: 5/1794: 6/1818
WILLIAM GEAKE 9/1876 — 35
WILLIAM HARRIS 8/1835 — 105, 108
WILLIAM MORGAN DAVIES 4/1857 — 105
WILLIAM PHILLIPS 10/1874
WILLIAM WEST 17/1846 — 56, 105, 108
WILN 4/1902
WINDSWORTH 1/1843 — 106, 109
WITCH 12/1816
WONDER 4/1887
YEOMAN'S GLORY 2/1813 — 106: 3/1826
YGDRASIL 5/1932
ZEPHYR 9/1794 — 10, 106: 3/1862
ZINGARI 4/1888 — 60, 62, 105
ZINGRA 8/1887
ZOE TREFFRY 10/1857
ZULEIKA 9/1848 — 107, 109

GENERAL INDEX

PAR DRY DOCK,

PAR, CORNWALL,

AUGUST 1st, 1896.

The following reduced prices will be charged after the above date.

		d.
Best hand picked Oakum, per lb.		$3\frac{1}{2}$
,, Stockholm Pitch	,,	$1\frac{1}{2}$
Galvanized Bolts	,,	$2\frac{1}{2}$
,, Deck Spikes	,,	$2\frac{3}{4}$
Common ditto	,,	2
Galvanized Nails, assorted	,,	$3\frac{1}{2}$
Common ditto	,,	$2\frac{1}{2}$

Men per day, 4/6.

Dock dues for Caulking Vessel from Keel to Gunwale from 35/- to 45/-.

Minimum Dock Dues 15/-

Maximum £5

Benjamin M. Tregaskes.

88   Par dry dock price list, 1896.